AF600422

THE CATHOLIC UNIVERSITY OF AMERICA
STUDIES IN CANON LAW
Number 71

The Approbation of Religious Institutes

A DISSERTATION

SUBMITTED TO THE FACULTY OF THE SCHOOL OF CANON LAW OF THE CATHOLIC UNIVERSITY OF AMERICA IN PARTIAL FULFILLMENT OF ITS REQUIREMENTS FOR THE DEGREE OF DOCTOR OF CANON LAW

BY

CLEMENT RAYMOND ORTH, O. M. C., J. C. L.,

Priest of the Order of Friars Minor Conventual,
Province of Our Lady of Consolation,
Louisville, Kentucky

CATHOLIC UNIVERSITY OF AMERICA
WASHINGTON, D. C.
1931

Nihil Obstat:
REV. LOUIS H. MOTRY, S.T.D., J.C.D.,
Censor Deputatus

Imprimi Permittitur:
FR. ALOYS M. FISH, O.M.C., Ph.D., S.T.D.,
Minister Provincialis.
Ludovicopoli, Ky., June 1, 1931.

Imprimatur:
✠ JOHN A. FLOERSH,
Ep. Ludovicopolitanus.
Louisville, Ky., June 3, 1931.

COPYRIGHT, 1931
by
THE CATHOLIC UNIVERSITY OF AMERICA
WASHINGTON, D. C.

Press of
Geo. G. Fetter Company, Inc.
Louisville, Ky.

To The

VERY REV. ALOYS M. FISH, O. M. C., PH. D., S. T. D.

Provincial of the Province of Our
Lady of Consolation

This Work
As a Token of Gratitude
Is Most Respectfully
Dedicated by the
Author

Table Of Contents

Foreword

The Catholic Church is holy. This quality which in the past has been her great characteristic, to this day is still her precious prerogative. As an aid to this holiness she has devised laws according to the needs of the times so that the faithful may be directed in an orderly manner to their proper end, which is personal sanctification. These canons or rules that she enacts are given in order to foster piety, to promote virtue, to correct disorders and to preserve discipline in the great society of the Church.

It is especially in her regulations laid down for religious institutes that the wisdom of the Church and her efforts to promote holiness are made manifest. The faithful in the world need guidance on the road to sanctification, but much more so do those favored souls require it, who are selected by God to seek out those higher paths to sanctity which are found in the religious state. The Church has established many and varied laws as a guide to these religious souls both as individuals and as organizations.

In order that a law may produce the beneficial results intended, it must be well known. In this work it is our intention to present to the reader a short history, summary and exposition of the laws laid down by the Church whereby she demands that those who desire to establish a new religious institute should first receive her approbation. The various canonical degrees of approbation which indicate stages in the life growth of a community, and also the methods of obtaining each form of approbation are likewise considered.

Foreword

The Church is a safe guide, and her experience of twenty centuries an invaluable acquisition. The promise of infallibility is an assurance that no harm can come through following her directions. In fact the great glory, renown, accomplishments, all that western monasticism can boast of must be attributed to the circumstance that it adhered to the See of Peter for guidance. It is evident that a lack of this dependence caused the weakness of eastern monasticism. By depending on Rome and taking their guidance from her the religious institutes of the Latin Church have been and are today one of the greatest instruments of moral good and of civilization in all parts of the world.

The author welcomes this opportunity to express his gratitude to the faculty of Canon Law of the Catholic University for their kind assistance during his course at the University. He also wishes to show his gratitude to Rev. Gerard Stauble, O. M. C., for his kind assistance in aiding him to prepare the work for publication.

CHAPTER 1

Article 1

Ecclesiastical Approbation in the First Four Centuries

Paganism had well-nigh reached its lowest level when Christ came into the world to save men. Through the establishment of His Church, Jesus Christ set up a standard whereby mankind once more could come to an appreciation and knowledge of its dignity. The doctrines of faith and the principles of morality which Christ taught and propagated in His three years of public ministry form the basis of the *depositum fidei* which the Church holds even in this twentieth century. The import of His message of truth and wisdom is clear and manifests the requisite means for personal santification. In no uncertain terms did He proclaim that whoever desired to partake of the fruits of His redemption must abide by His teachings. Throughout His life Jesus Christ stressed the necessity of a faithful fulfillment of the commandments, and, additionally, instituted means for man to aid him in the individual work of his salvation.

In very clear words, however, does He assure us that there are further means open to those who desire more closely to imitate and love Him. Besides His commandments He gave the evangelical counsels to lead men to the higher road of perfection. Thus it is written in St. Matthew[1] that a man once asked of Jesus the following question, "Good Master, what shall I do that I may have life everlasting?" The answer was, "If

[1] xix, 16-21.

thou wilt enter into life, keep the commandments." But when the young man replied that he had done so from his youth, Jesus said to him, "If thou wilt be perfect, go sell what thou hast and give to the poor, and thou shalt have treasure in heaven: and come follow Me." In this passage the two diverse states in the messianic kingdom on earth are briefly described; the first being imposed upon all, the second suggested to those who desire a closer following of Christ.[2] Christ Himself describes this second mode of life as the state of perfection, "if thou wilt be perfect". All authors see in these words and other related passages[3] the germ of the religious state. In these, the three evangelical counsels of poverty, chastity and obedience have their root. The advice to sell all plainly inculcates the poverty of Christ; that of following Him, the counsels of perfect chastity and obedience which were necessary in order to follow Him during His earthly career.

When one speaks of the religious state one refers to a condition of life which has these three as a foundation and which is principally motivated by them and embraced and followed by various persons or societies in the Church. From the time when our Lord drew His first Apostles to Himself and requested them to leave their nets and follow Him[4] there have never been wanting in any age holy men and women who, feeling the impulse to a higher life and eager to draw closer to their Savior, have voluntarily added these counsels to the precepts as a motive and reason of their lives. These holy men and women have never been lacking in the Church,[5] and there have been thousands in all ages who form an unbroken line linking the vocation of the Apostles in Galilee with the

---

[2] Cornely, *Comm. in Evang. secundum Matthaeum*, Pars altera, p. 163; Currier, Charles, *History of Rel. Orders*, p. 7; Wernz, *Jus Decretalium*, III, n. 599; Heimbucher, *Die Orden und Kongregationen*, I, 17.

[3] Luke, XIV, 26; I Corinthians, VII, 25. sq.

[4] Matth., IV, 22.

[5] Suarez, *De Religiosis*, L. XIII, c. 4, n. 11, tom. III; Wernz, *Jus Decretalium*, III, n. 601; Concilium prov. Pragensis (1860)—*Collectio Lac.* V, 570-571; Bouix, *De Regularibus*, pp. 146-159. This last mentioned author goes to great lengths to show that the first Christians who had their goods in common were true religious.

present time. In fact, it was well nigh impossible to conceive that the counsels of Christ could have been given in vain.[6] Following in the footsteps of her Master, the Church has ever approved of these holy souls and encouraged them in their endeavor, to lead the more perfect life. She would be untrue to the trust committed to her care if she did otherwise, or if she were to proscribe the state which leads to greater sanctification since her sole *raison d'etre* is to make men holy.

But the experience of centuries has made her wise in the ways of God and men and has made known to her that not all which has an appearance of good is such in reality. Time has made her realize that under the guise of zeal, error and heresy often lurk; that unrestricted zeal causes disturbances in the social order; that the too great miltiplication of institutes may often-times not produce the holiness for which this evangelical life is intended. Thus as the years pass she sees it fitting to guide this growth and to mould the character of the religious state in such forms as to adapt it to the capabilities of men and yet leave it as a high road to perfection. With this end in view it has been decreed that those desirous of establishing such a life in community should have her permission and approval.

Many attempts are made to prove that Christ and His Apostles were the first true religious, that the monastic life was therefore formed in the very beginning of Christianity. Yet history does not show such to be the case. It is easy to conceive that many Christians, immediately after the death of our Lord, led a life which in some part at least partook of the nature of the religious state. Inspired by the word of Christ many pious women led a life of perfect chastity; others, men and women, sold all their goods; and for a time the Christians of Jerusalem used everything in common.[7] Still there are no records at hand to show that the Apostles, or their first successors, endeavored to found communities

[6] Concilium Vaticanum, Schema reformatum constitutionis dogmaticae de doctrina catholica, cap. XV,—*Coll. Lac.* VII, 575 d.

[7] Acts, II, 44.

which had as their essence the practice of the evangelical counsels in their entirety. On the contrary the evidence seems to indicate that individuals practiced one or the other counsel and asumed other mortifications without, however, leaving their homes and the world.[8] And surely had the Apostles contemplated such a thing it would have been generally impossible to put it into effect because of the chaotic conditions of the times, for everywhere from the beginning of their mission persecutions and civil suppression formed their invariable lot. This does not preclude the fact that many, who were distinguished by the name *ascetics* did live a real life of perfection.[9] Some of the greatest men of the early church are enumerated among these ascetics or confessors of the faith as they were also called.[10]

The Church through the individual bishops encouraged this practice of asceticism, yet there are no indications of her having taken the initiative or that she placed all these souls under her special charge. In fact, the mode of life must be chiefly ascribed to the personal efforts of individuals, who used this as a means to overcome temptation and to lead a more perfect life. It should ever be kept in mind that the history of the Church during the first three hundred years is the history of her struggle for existence. Persecutions succeeded one another in rapid succession so that the Church had few opportunities to organize and form communities. To understand her situation, proscribed as she was by Roman Law which at that time embraced the known world, one has only to portray a mental picture of similar modern conditions when the Church was vehemently persecuted and religious life forbidden in Eng-

[8] Funk, *Manual of Church History*, I, 209; Suarez, *De Religiosis*, L. III, c. 3, n. 3 and 4.

[9] Bertrand Conway. Christian Asceticism in the First Three Centuries, *Cath. World*, 98 (1914), 772-789, proves conclusively that the early asceticism was truly Christian in origin and nature and so does not owe its origin to Buddhism or any other similar paganistic forms. Vicente, *Instituta Recentia*, p. 3; Toso, *Commentaria Minora*, II: *De Personis*, p. 5.

[10] Vermeersch, *De Religiosis*, II, p. 5, mentions St. Clement of Rome, St. Ignatius of Antioch, St. Polycarp, St. Athanasius, and St. John Chrysostom as being of their number.

land, Germany, France and Russia, and then it will be realized how impossible it was to form religious communities whilst the persecution of Rome raged and destroyed.

It is only towards the end of the third century that we find traces of religious life which bears some resemblance to our own modern conception of this state and in which the religious profession becomes by degrees perfected and brought under rule.[11] The reasons for the phenomenal growth at this time are to be sought in the bitter persecutions and in the decadence of the morals of the times. For when fire and sword were rampant in the land and when the fury of the basest elements of Rome was at its height, certain holy men fled to the solitude of the desert for that safety of soul and body which was denied to them amongst men. Thus began the glorious history of these renowned men whose lives of holiness and austerity have been the everlasting glory of the Church. Of this number St. Paul, the Hermit, (250-356) is considered the head,[12] and the first of whom we have any record to embrace this evangelical life of perfection in the desert. In quick succession others followed his example and thus the early years of the hermitic life can boast of such glorious names as Sts. Anthony, Macarius, Pacome, Ammons and Simon Stylites. In time communities were organized, of which the first leader seems to have been St. Pacome, who is said to have introduced common life to the anchorites of the Egyptian desert.[13] He it was who brought rule and order to monastic life. It is also said of him that he founded eight monasteries, over each of which he placed an abbot. Later prominent leaders in community life were Sts. Palaemon, Hilarion, Basil, Martin, Augustine, Benedict, Thecla, and Massilla.

[11] Vermeersch, A., "Religious Life," *Cath. Encycl.*, XII, 750.

[12] Heimbucher, *Die Orden und Kongregation*, I. 32; Philip Vering, *Corpus Jur. Eccl.*, p. 685; Wernz, *Jus Decretalium*, III, n. 602; Vecchiotti, *Inst. Can.*, L. II. c. 9, 88, p. 365; Funk, *op. cit.*, I, 210; Balmes, *European Civilization*, p. 231. The last mentioned author says that the number of these solitaries was so great that it would seem incredible were it not vouched for by men worthy of the highest respect.

[13] Heimbucher, *op. cit.*, I, 37; Philip Vering, *op. cit.*, p. 685; Raus *De Sacrae Obedientiae Virtute et Voto*, n. 78. p. 143.

The monastic life which had so small a beginning in the deserts of Egypt soon spread to all parts of the Christian world, to Sicily, Syria, Palestine, Cyprus, Gaul, and Rome. But seldom does one hear of these foundations being made through the authority of the local bishop or any other ecclesiastical power. In practically all cases the foundations were by private initiative. Not that these men had the intention to found religious communities, as the later founders did, but often-times against the will of the founder cicumstances forced the foundation of communities. The sanctity and austerity of their lives had gone forth among people and had attracted numerous disciples who endeavored to emulate these masters of perfection, to be their followers as the disciples were of our Lord. These founders had left the world solely for the purpose of drawing closer to God by meditation, penance and seclusion and had no intention of being concerned directly with the welfare of others. Their sole motive in entering the desert was to remove all impediments to their life of sanctity, to avoid the allurements, enticements and temptations of the world. But once having drawn a large following it is easy to understand how these great masters of the desert were forced to draw up rules and regulations for the ordering of such a large number of men, as otherwise grave disorders woud have resulted. This is the only logical and historical explanation for the formation of these cenobitic communities.

Viewing the first four centuries of early Christian religious life in the light of historical fact it is easily seen why no general legislation was passed demanding that these men receive permission of some ecclesiastical authority before the formation of such communities. Above all this was the formative period of the Church and she was busy not so much with law as with teaching. The fervor and charity of these Christians was especially so great that very few laws were needed for their guidance. Besides, the persecutions closely followed one another, and always waxed stronger, so that the Church's main concern was to preserve her children to the faith. Lastly history teaches that laws are the expression of the experience of the society enacting them. They are not merely theoretical, to avoid possibilities that never have occurred before, but rather are placed as statutes to correct existing evils and to prevent their recurrence. As long then as no harm was done to society or to the members of the communities, or no errors or heretical forms of life were propagated by these religious, they were not restricted in any manner nor was it required by any general law that they have any episcopal consent or sanction to form communities.

The first law of which there exists any record declaring the necessity of the bishop's permission before a religious house or community could be established is found in the canons of the Council of Chalcedon (451). Before this time no general positive law of the Church demanded such permission. The foundation for this statement is based on the absence of any record of similar previous legislation. But monasticism, born in the desert, in its phenomenal growth soon came more and more into contact with cities and villiages. It was bound to come in touch with many local bishops, especially in places where monasteries were being constructed. While the majority of monks remained faithful, still there were some who did not retain their first fervor, and accordingly, many abuses crept in. To aggravate the evil many leaving their solitary life roamed about from place to place causing much disorder. Because their life was highly honored by the people the monks were often led to judge themselves superior to the people and even above the bishops. Several Councils, both general and particular, before Chalcedon declared that the bishops had power over these monks, to regulate their affairs and to see that they preached no errors.[14] The civil law of this time 390 also saw fit to lay down regulations for the monks, especially demanding that they keep from wandering about in cities.[15]

[14] Nicene Council, c. 56; Conway, Bertrand L., "Christian Asceticism in the First Three Centuries," *Cath. World,* 98 (1914), 777, 784.

[15] Theodosian Code, IX, 40, 16; XI, 30, 57; XVI, II, I; XVI, 3, 1, has: *"Quicunque sub professione monachi reperiuntur, deserta loca et vastas solitudines sequi atque habitare jubeantur."*

That the bishop had power to lay down particular laws for his own diocese requiring his permission before a new monastery could be built is quite certain. His power over all in the diocese was generally recognized before the year 400. History relates that St. Martin of Tours asked leave of the Bishop of Potiers in 360 to found a Monastery in that city.[16] St. Augustine was always accustomed to begin a monastery only with the consent of the bishop of the place where the monks were to live. [17] Besides many cases are in evidence where the bishops themselves founded monastic institutes, as was the case with Sts. Basil, Eligius, Bishop of Tournay, and Germain, Bishop of Auxerre.[18] These few examples are an indication of a general recognition of the supervision of bishops in the establishment of monastic institutes. Permission seems to have been sought not necessarily because of any particular laws but because of the desire of co-operation with the bishops and also for the purpose of placing the societies under his guidance and protection.

Article II

The Council of Chalcedon

In order to understand more clearly the laws demanding ecclesiastical approbation before a religious institute could be founded it is important to grasp the historical divisions of that legislation. For the sake of convenience it is divided into four parts, exclusive of the time before the Council of Chalcedon which lacks any legislation on this point. The first period extends from the Council of Chalcedon (451) to the IV Lateran Council (1215); the second, from the IV Lateran Council to the Council of Trent (1545-1563); the third, from the Council of Trent to Leo XIII (1900); the fourth from 1900 to the present day.

[16] Montalembert, *Monks of the West,* I, 340.

[17] Van Espes, *Opera Omnia,* T. I, pars I, tit. 24, c. 3; Lyons, *The Erection* and Suppression of Religious Houses, p. 16.

[18] Verhoefen, *De Regularibus,* I, p. 476; Montalembert. *op. cit.* I, 359.

It is to this, the Council of Chalcedon (451), the fourth General Council of the Church, that we owe the first legislation requiring that all foundations of religious institutes be under ecclesiastical authorization. The primary purpose of the Council was the condemnation of Eutychianism[19] and its acts refer principally to discussions on this subject. The fact that Eutyches was a monk[20] and that many of his brethren, led by a certain John who was also a priest[21] defended Eutyches, no doubt caused many of the Fathers present to deem some legislation necessary to protect the monks from heresy and to keep them under the subjection of their bishops. Eutyches and his monks had, as Eutychians, withdrawn themselves from the jurisdiction of their bishops whom they had charged with heresy.[22]

Strange to say, at least so it appears in our days, the petition seeking for control of the establishment of monastic houses was not presented by the Fathers of the Council but by Marcian, the Emperor, who was present at the conferences and, in recommending their adoption, presented certain decrees to the Fathers.[23] His request reads thus:

Quaedam sunt, quae ad honorem vestrae reverentiae vobis fervovimus decorem esse judicantes, a vobis haec regulariter potius formari per Synodum, guam nostri legi sanciri; and the first canon suggested by him is as follows:

Eos qui vere et sincere solitariam arripiscent vitam, debito honore dignos judicamus. Quoniam vero quidam sub praetextu solitariae vitae et ecclesias et communes perturbant causas; placuit nullum quidem aedificare monasterium praeter voluntatem episcopi civitatis .... Eos vero monachos, qui per singulas civitates sunt atque provincias subjici episcopo.[24]

---

[19] Novel, 131, 1; Parsons, *Studies in Church History*, I, 332; Tanquerey, *Synopsis Theologiae Dogmaticae* I, 602.
[20] Mansi, VI. 762.
[21] Mansi, VI. 778.
[22] Hefele, *History of the Councils*. III, 390.
[23] Parsons, *Studies in Church History*, I, 333.
[24] Actio 6—Mansi, VII, 174.

The Fathers willingly acceded to his request, and probably would have acted without his suggestion. The law was promulgated in the fifteenth action where a summary of the canons previously decreed at the Council was made. Thus in canon four:

Qui vere et sincere monasticam vitam aggrediuntur digni convenienti honore habeantur. Quoniam autem nonnulli monachi praetextu utentes, et ecclesias et negotia civilia perturbant, et temere citra ullam discriminis rationem, in urbibus circumcursantes, quin etiam monasteria sibi constituere studentes, visum est, nullum usquam aedificare nec constituere posse monasterium vel oratorium domum, praeter sententiam ipsius civitatis episcopi: monachos autem qui sunt in unaquaque regione et civitate episcopo subjectos esse.[23]

The first fact drawn from the law and the emperor's request is that monasteries were gradually being built away from the solitude of the desert and near the cities. With this change in environment came laxity and diminished fervor whereby many of the monks became tainted with worldliness and, wandering about from place to place, caused many disturbances. Many also found an irksomeness in living subject to their own superiors and so started monasteries or cells of their own. Some other monks adopted false opinions and fell into dogmatical errors and by the propagation of these heretical tenets gravely harmed both Church and State. Thus it became apparent that if these disturbances in the civil and ecclesiastical realms were to be quieted the monasteries should be in the power of those who could keep them free from error and excess, who could control them and regulate the proper observance of the vows and at the same time regulate their growth with

[23] Mansi, VII, 359. This differs in wording but not in sense from another version given by Mansi (VIII, 394), which reads thus: "Quoniam vero quidam sub praextextu habitu monachi ecclesias, et conventus et res communes disturbant, civitates circumeuntes indiscrete, necnon et monasteria sibi constituere studentes, placuit, ut nullum eorum usquam aedificare liceat, neque monasterium constituere, neque oratorium absque civitatis episcopi voluntate." Other regulations concerning monks were also put in force at this time, thus canon 7 forbade monks to return to the world; canon 16 forbade marriage. Cf. Funk, *Manual of Church History*, I, 212.

due regard for the social order. Because of the many heresies prevalent the ecclesiastical authorities were inclined to be somewhat suspicious of asceticism.[26] The danger of Manichaeism was always imminent and these monks, judging themselves a superior type of Christian in many cases, were apt to prove a source of disorder. They were truly popular with the masses and did not fail in some instances to use their influence against both the ecclesiastical and the civil powers. This popularity may explain why the emperor in presenting his decrees considered that the Church laws would prove of more value than any he could make.

The general mind of the Council in making not only this law but also others concerning religious was to give the bishop full authority over all monks. From the wording of the canon it seems that it was entirely a new legislation, for indiscrete building, was causing concern to the bishops and no hint is made of any illiceity of the acts. The word *usquam* shows the extent of the prohibition as to locality, for it was to hold everywhere whether in the city or country. As far as territorial extent is concerned one needs but recall that the Council of Chalcedon was a General Council of the Church, and therefore, its dogmatic and disciplinary decrees were binding on the universal church. Thus for the establishment of each new monastery the permission of the local Ordinary, for in that sense the word "bishop" must be understood,[27] was required and also sufficient. The building of a new monastery in that age was generally synonymous with the beginning of a new institute. For monasteries did not form a part of a grand unit as they often do today, but each was independent and formed a distinct religious community. Directly applicable to religious houses the law thus indirectly forbade the founding of a new religious institute without the bishop's consent, as a community was not thought of without existing in houses, and since no house could be built without the assent of the bishop neither

[26] W. G. deBurgh, *The Legacy of the Ancient World.* p. 320, footnote.
[27] Rittershutii, *Expositio Methodica Novellarum Imp. Justiniani,* Pars I, c. 6, n. 33.

could a new religious body be organized without his due permission.

The action of the Emperor at Chalcedon gives an insight into the close and intimate union of Church and State at that time. This was, in part at least, a remnant of the paganistic days when the rulers used the prevalent religion as a tool of the State. At the conversion of the Emperor Constantine, the Catholic faith received official state recognition and later on was acknowledged as the, religion of the state.[28] In the majority of cases, with good intent, he and his successors took it upon themselves to defend the faith and protect the Church. In many cases their help proved embarrassing to the Church, as not infrequently they proposed errors and heresy for adoption. The decree in this case is disciplinary and under the conditions it was not considered improper for the Emperor Marcian to propose it.

This union of Church and State is vividly exemplified in the *Codex Juris Civilis* of Justinian. His laws contain many that are purely ecclesiastical in character, and also many that were passed in synods, particular and general. The Emperor's maxim was that the salvation of the State and the individual depended on the Church's beng maintained in its integrity.[29] He made no effort to intrude on the domain of the Church since he regarded it as having sovereign juridical personality,[31] but rather tried to supplement the work of the Church. It was with this purpose in mind that the power of the bishop was strengthened and the monastic life minutely regulated.[32]

Nor were the Popes always adverse to this help from civil authorities, as they oftentimes petitioned this help. So Pope Simplicius writing to the Emperor Zeno in 477, requested him to order that the statutes of the Chalcedon Synod should be inviolately enforced.[33] Justinian's law is of particular interest

[28] Buckland, *Textbook of Roman Law,* p. 179. Code, I, 1, 2.
[29] Holmes, *Age of Justinian and Theodora,* II, p. 689.
[31] Brown, *Canonical Juristic Personality,* p. 33.
[32] Holmes, *op. cit.,* II, 690-691.
[33] Andreas Thiel, *Epistolae Romanorum Pontificum Genuinae,* I, 189.

here because he saw fit to incorporate the law of Chalcedon regarding religious houses in his compilation, which reads:

Illud igitur ante alia dicendum est, ut omni tempore et in omni terra nostra, si quis aedificare venerabile monasterium voluerit, non prius licentiam esse hoc agendi, quam deo amabilem locorum episcopum advocet, at ille manus extendat ad coelum et per orationem locum consecret deo, figens in eo nostrae salutis signum (dicimus autem adorandam et honorandam vere crucem), sicque incohet aedificium, bonum utique quoddam hoc et decens fundamentum ponens. Hoc itaque principium piae venerabilium monasteriorum fabricae fiat.[34]

His words are a very strong confirmation of the Council of Chalcedon, and through this statute the civil law assumed the position of helper to the Church. But in this decree much more is implied. Any monastery established without the Bishop's sanction would not receive recognition before the law, and this recognition was of practical value especially when legacies, donations and the like were in question. In another place Justinian implies the illegal status of a monastery built without the knowledge of the Ordinary. After having repeated the previous law he concludes: "*Multi enim simulantes fabricare quasi orationis domus medentur languoribus, non orthodoxarum ecclesiarum aedificatores facti, sed speluncarum illicitarum.*"[35] While in this passage the monasteries are not mentioned, yet when it is considered that they are mentioned in the earlier part of this number the latter term would also apply to them under the same circumstances.

There is this aspect then to the prohibition of the State and Church that a monastery built without the consent of the local Ordinary could not have any juristic personality. Roman

[34] Novel. V, 1. This canon is repeated in an indirect shorter form in Nov. 131, 7. "Si quis autem voluerit fabricare venerabile oratorium aut monasterium, non aliter inchoandam fabricam, nisi locorum sanctissimus episcopus orationem ibi fecerit et venerabilem fixerit crucem." Indirectly also in 131, 1, where it is stated that the rules of the first four general Councils have the force of law in the empire.

[35] Novel. 67, 1.

law recognized corporations and after Constantine the Church was thus acknowledged, as also were dioceses and apparently monasteries.[36] For besides three persons and a scope[37] it was necessary for legal personality that a thing be legally established through the approbation of the State.[38] Authorities differ as to whether the permission of the State was the creative act without which the corporation could not exist;[39] but all agree that no corporation could exist against the will of the State when it was expressly forbidden.[40] And however much one may argue about its existence before actual condemnation, still one is forced to admit that no monastery could civilly exist except through the proper ecclesiastical authority. In the eyes of the State the unauthorized buildings were considered as the gathering places of heretics whose meetings were severely prohibited.[41] These refer only to civil effects and held only where the Roman law was in force. This is one of many instances of the incorporation of ecclesiastical laws into civil laws, and shows the great lengths that the State employed to strengthen and increase the authority of the bishops.

This enactment by the Council of Chalcedon concerning the erection of monasteries became from that time on part of the law of Christendom.[42] Its influence was felt in the numerous and repeated legislation of succeeding Councils. Thus the Council of Constantinople confirmed it decrees;[43] the Council of Barcelona, Spain, refers explicily to the decrees of Chalcedon;[44] and the Trullan Council (692) declared its dis-

[36] Buckland, *Textbook of Roman Law,* p. 180.
[37] Dig. 50, 16, 85.
[38] Frederico Carlo di Savigny, *Sistema del Diritto Romano Attuale,* II, 278; Buckland, *op. cit.,* 179.
[39] Brown, *Canonical Juristic Personality,* p. 66.
[40] Brown, *op. cit.,* p. 67.
[41] Code, 1, 5, 3 and 5; Code 1, 5, 8, 3.
[42] Montalembert, *Monks of the West,* I, 219.
[43] Mansi, VII, 1179.
[44] Mansi, IX, 109.
[45] Hefele, *History of the Councils,* V, 224. This Trullan Council is still the guide for religious of the Greek Ruthenian rite. Cf. Visosevic, "De Disciplina monastica apud Catholicas ritus graco-slavici," *Comm. pro. Rel.,* VIII (1927), 212.

ciplinary measures were still in force.[45] Numerous other councils show by their adoption of certain regulations that they used this Council of Chalcedon as a guide.

It is, however, chiefly in the Church of the West that numerous repetitions of this law are found from the sixth century on. This is particularly noticeable of the Church in Gaul which was at this time in a flourishing condition. All the particular Councils which legislate for religious follow the familiar legislation of Chalcedon.[46] The Councils of other countries are not so explicit as those of France. In the Council of Barcelonia, Spain (540), the legislation of Chalcedon is restated in a general way in canon 10, which says: "De monachis vero id observari praecipimus quae Synodus Calcedonensis constituit."[47] The Council of Toledo (694), in canon 11 uses the exact wording of the decree of Epaon which was given above.[48]

In later Councils the power of bishops over monasteries is taken for granted. So in the year 619, St. Isidore of Seville held a Provincial Synod in which he decreed: "The newly erected monasteries in the provice of Boetica are confirmed,"[49] thus signifying they had been previously approved and also

---

[46] Montalembert, *Monks of the West*, I, 452. Thus the Council of Agde (506) has in canon 27: "Monasterium novum, nisi episcopo, aut permittente, aut probante, nullus incipere aut fundare praesumat."—Mansi VII, 329; while canon 58 contains the words: "Cellulas novas, aut congregatiunculas monachorum absque notitia episcopi prohibemus institui." Mansi, VII, 331. Only five years later the Council of Orleans (511) passed a similar law which is found in canon 32: "Nullus monachus, congregatione monasteria derelicta, ambitionis et vanitatis impulsu, cellulam construere sine episcopi permissione, vel abbatis sui voluntate praesumat."—Mansi, VIII, 347. In the year 517 the same prohibition is found in canon 10 of the Council of Epaon. "Cellas novas, aut congregatiunculas monachorum absque episcopi notitia prohibemus institui."—Mansi, VIII, 560. The same canon has for its title, "Ut nova monasteria sine episcopi notitia non fiant." —Mansi, VIII, 588. Finally in 524 at the Council of Lerida the canons of the preceding Councils are reaffirmed in these words of canon 3: "De monachis vero id observari placuit quod Synodus Agathensis, Aurelianensis noscitur decrevisse."—Mansi, VIII, 613. It must be kept in mind that very many other laws were passed with regard to religious in these Synods.

[47] Mansi, IX, 109.

[48] Mansi, XII. 105.

[49] Canon 10—Mansi, X, 555.

supposing power to approve. In England no specific reference is found referring to the necessity of episcopal approbation, though many other canons of Chalcedon are referred to and enforced.[50] There the Councils were concerned more with the regulation of the internal affairs of the monasteries, taking the power of the bishops over them for granted.

The main reason why all this legislation seemed so necessary and why it was so often repeated at these various particular councils must be ascribed to the desire of the bishops to bring out a general law to more particular notice. Often particular councils incorporate general laws in order to call more attention to them and assure a better observance. The bishops used these means to promulgate a general law which probably was not so well known on account of the circumstances of the times. In some few instances troubles similar to those which the Eastern bishops had experienced may have been the lot of some of the Western bishops also, and thus evinced the necessity of a rigorous enforcement of this legislation. For often when particular councils find it necessary to repeat the legislation of a general council it is because the general law has not always been properly observed in that locality.

History, however, is silent and tells us little explicitly concerning the observance of the decree of Chalcedon. Montalembert admits there were numerous violations of this law and ascribes this as the cause of the decay of Eastern monasticism.[51] Whether the strict observance or a general non-observance prevailed in the East is hard to say. History teaches this decree had been incorporated into the law of the Roman Empire, the center of which was in the East, and so it had the sanction of both the civil and ecclesiastical authorities. This civil law continued in force for many centuries, even after the West became separated from the East. Besides the power of the bishops in the East was well established over the monasteries

[50] *Exceptiones Eggberti Eborancensis Archiepiscopi*—Mansi, XII, 414.
[51] *Monks of the West*, I, 219.

at this period, and for this reason alone it seems hardly probable that the law was entirely ignored. Only the Trullan Council and that of Constantinople in the East mention the legislation of Chalcedon in later years, whereas in the West numerous particular councils repeatedly refer to this decree. One may interpret such a fact in various ways and so this consideration alone does not lead to any definite conclusion.

Thus wherever the Catholic religion flourished, whether in the East or West, the necessity of episcopal consent was recognized as necessary for the establishment of any religious community. Where Christianity was yet to be propagated monasteries were generally built long before the establishment of any bishopric, for the monks working among pagans, established their monasteries wherever they founded settlements in pagan countries. It so happened that in many cases these monasteries were the cradles of bishoprics. For in England and Wales every bishopric was cradled in a monastery.[52] In such cases the power of these religious missionaries was similar to that of the bishops. But once a bishop was lawfully appointed over a district he alone had complete authority over the establishment of any new religious community in his diocese.

During all these years, until the IV Lateran Council (1215), it was sufficient to receive the permission of the bishop, and no papal affirmation or approval was required by law. Nowhere do we read that Sts. Anthony, Basil, Augustine, or Benedict applied for pontifical approbation of their institutes, and precisely for the reason that no law demanded this.[53] However, many instances of papal approbation of religious institutes are in evidence, but these are always cases of already established communities obtaining approval of their mode of life, or applying to Rome for this approbation as a greater protection against the savage inroads of the numerous wandering tribes of the times.

---

[52] Montalembert, *op. cit.*, II, 1.

[53] Bellarminus, L. II. *De Monachis*, c. 4; Schmalzgrüber, *Jus Ecclesiasticum, De Regularibus*, Lib. III, Pars III, tit. 31, n. 22; Suarez, *De Religiosis*, T. III, L. 2, c. 17, n. 9.

Sometimes, and this most frequently, it was done for the sake of greater honor and stability, or also to obtain independence and freedom from the jurisdiction of the bishop.[54] Examples of papal recognition could be multiplied, as about the ninth and tenth centuries it became an almost universal custom for all monasteries [55] once they were in a flourishing condition, to obtain the Pope's confirmation because of the privileges and favors that thereby accrued to the monasteries, and because of the honor that was conferred through recognition by the greatest power in Christendom. Later the Pope frequently approved the Constitutions of religious orders by solemn letters.[56]

When the term "episcopal" or "papal approbation" is used in reference to this period of history one should not make the mistake of confounding it with all that the word connotes today. By the Council of Chalcedon only the permission of the bishop was required. But in view of the purpose of the law no doubt he examined thoroughly the founder's motives and plan of life, especially regarding any probable heresies in his maner of life. Yet the daily life of the monks, especially the rules and regulations were not subject to such exact scrutiny on the part of the bishop. The formation of these rules was left entirely to the founder, nor do we read anywhere that any of the earlier rules were approved explicitly by any ecclesiastical power. There was no such thought of a formal

[54] Thus the monastery of Bobbio had trouble with its bishop and Bertulph, the Abbot at the time, went to Rome and obtained the Pope's sovereign approbation. Cf. Montalembert, *Monks of the West*, I, 583. Also in 602, the Burgundian king, Brunebart, sent ambassadors to Rome to obtain the Pope's confirmation of two monasteries which he had founded at Autun. Montalembert, *op. cit.*, I, 382. When Monte Cassino was destroyed (580) by the Lombards, the monks fled to Rome and Pelagius II gave them a hearty reception permitting them to build a monastery near the Lateran Bascilica. Cf. Roger Hudleston, "Monte Cassino," *Cath. Encyc.*, X, 527. Pope Zachary in 751 wrote a letter to Boniface, the Archbishop, conferring certain privileges on the Abbacy of Fulda, "which," he said, "was built by you."

[55] Bondini. *De Privilegio Exemptionis*, p. 8.

[56] Alexander III in a bull confirmed the military institute of St. James de Spatha in Spain in 1175. Cf. *Bullarium Romanum*, II, 782. He also confirmed by a bull the rules and constitutions of the Cistercians in 1181. *Bullarium Rom.*, II, 833. Cf. also *A. S. S.*, 35, 385.

or explicit approbation as we have now,[57] though it is probable that some approbation was give to the rules.[58] Whatever approbation the Ordinaries gave should be considered as rather tacit, that is, having been acquainted with these rules and seeing their benefits they placed no obstacle in the way, allowing them to be used by the monks as a guide of life. The life was approved of because of the high ideals and motives animating these founders and not so much that every detail had been carefully examined and minutely scrutinized so as to produce a rule of life sufficient for the needs of that society.

As far as papal approbation was concerned, it was merely tacit. The Popes saw these institutes, realized their good to the individuals, the Church, and society and as such praised them and ever heaped honors on them. There are many cases of explicit approbation by special declaration but these were given only on request of an institute and generally when it had been well established.

Meanwhile under the wholesome and extensive legislation of the Council of Chalcedon and particular councils of the succeeding centuries, Western monasticism grew by leaps and bounds. Whereas already in 363, monasticism had reached the peak of development in the East,[59] it was not till the sixth century that it reached its fullest development in the West.[60] Amidst the ruins of the fallen Roman Empire, monasticism raised its head and was instrumental in building up a new civilization. It was St. Benedict who gave the greatest impulse to Western monasticism. In 529 he laid the foundation of his

[57] Vicente, *Instituta Recentia*, n. 28, p. 13; Fanfani, *De Jure Religiosorum;* p. 6. Piat, *Praelectiones Jur. Reg.*, I. q. 19; Wernz, *Jus Decretalium*, III, n. 590.
[58] Saurez, *De Rel.*, III, L. II, c. 17, n. 4.
[59] Currier, *History of Rel. Orders*, p. 4.
[60] Currier, *op. cit.*, p. 6.

order[61] which during the succeeding ages has been a crown of glory to the Church. In the meantime monasteries were multiplied, either through example, through the diligence of the monks, or through the invitations of people and rulers.[62] His order soon spread beyond the Italian peninsula to other countries, namely to Sicilia 534, France 543, and Spain about a century later, later to Frisia and in the beginning of the eighth century to Germany through the efforts of St. Boniface.[63] Whilst the Order of St. Benedict was doing its great work, Ireland also had its St. Columban who founded many monasteries there and also established the great monastery of Luxeil in France about the year 590.[64]

For centuries the Orders did wonderful work in the Church. When from man's proneness to laxity they were threatened with destruction and decay, God at sundry times raised up men to combat the evil and recall the monks to their early fervor.[65] Thus St. Benedict of Aniane (821) by his zeal and his Concordance of Rules helped in the reformation of various monasteries. Likewise of great renown is the reform of Cluny by St. Odo, the Abbot (927-942). This had such great influence that in the beginning of the twelfth century there were two thousand monasteries under the abbot of Cluny.[66]

In the eleventh century St. Bernard reformed the Cistercians. The same century also witnessed a revival of many of the old orders whilst various new orders also arose.[67] Thus in

[61] Heimbucher, *Die Orden and Kongregationen,* I, 97. Efforts have been made to show that Pope Gregory the Great approved the rule of St. Benedict. That he praised it publicly is certain but he did this as a wise and holy doctor of the Church. It is said that he approved it orally and that Pope Zachary later confirmed this, still historical proof is lacking for asserting this. It is reasonable that Popes should find words of praise for the wisdom displayed in the rule, but this must be duly distinguished from approval. Cf. Suarez, *De Rel.,* III, L. II, c. 17, n. 11.

[62] Suarez, *De Rel.,* L. II, c. 15, n. 17.

[63] Currier, *History of Religious Orders,* p. 6.

[64] Currier, *op. cit.,* p. 7.

[65] Vermeersch, *De Rel. Institutis et Personis,* I, n. 44, p. 33.

[66] Vermeersch, *op. cit.,* I, n. 44, p. 34; Currier, *op. cit.,* p. 8.

[67] *Vermeersch, De Rel. Institutis et Personis,* I, n. 44, p. 34; Currier, *op. cit.,* p. 8.

1012 St. Romuald laid the foundations of the Camaldolese. He was shortly followed by St. John Gualbert (1038), who established the Order of Vallombrosa. The Carthusians received their spirit from St. Bruno who founded the Monastery of Chartreaux in 1084, and the Abbacy of Citeaux in 1098. The Premonstratensians and the Order of Monte Virgine arose in 1119. The wars against the Mohammedans caused the rise of numerous military orders and others devoted to the redemption and the alleviation of the sufferings of captives. This period produced the following orders: the Knight Hospitallers of St. John, the Templars, the Teutonic Knights, Alcantara, the Order of the Blessed Trinity for the Redemption of Captives, and Our Lady of Mercy.[68] Directly, the Church had not initiated this growth, yet her guiding hand is discernible in directing this expansion to its most useful form, for only through encouragement from ecclesiastical authorities was such a wholesome growth possible.

That the legislation of Chalcedon concerning the foundation of religious houses had not been changed before 1215 is quite clear from the collection of laws by Gratian and from the Basilica. For when Gratian compiled his famous Concordiam Discordantium Canonum[69] the law was recognized as still in force. He repeats the substance of the earlier law in these words:

Quidam monachorum habitu utentes indifferenter per civitates incedunt, necnon et monasteria, et seipsos praesumptione propria commendant. Placuit igitur neminem aut aedificare, aut construere monasteria, aut oratorii domum sine conscientia ipsius civitatis episcopi . . . . Eos vero, qui ausi fuerint rescindere hujusmodi institutionem quocumque modo . . . si quidem fuerint clerici pro personarum ordinatione subiaceant condemnationibus canonum: si vero laici, vel monachi fuerint,

[68] Currier, *History of Religious Orders*, p. 11.

[69] Blat, *Normae Generales*, I, p. 33, gives the year of compilation as between 1130-1150. Augustine, *Commentary on Canon Law*, I, p. 35, places it between 1150-1151, but admits the impossibility of setting any certain date.

communione priventur."[10] And the next canon has, "Monasterium quoque absque episcopi permissione nulli incipere aut fundare liceat."[11] Later he also quotes the already mentioned canons of Agde and Orleans.

Two centuries earlier the same law had also been included in the Basilica[12] in these words:

Sancimus, ut quocumque imperii nostri loco, si quis venerabile monasterium aedificare voluerit, non prius ei hoc faciendi potestas sit, quam Dei amantissimum loci Episcopum advocaverit, atque his manibus ad coelum extensis . . . . Hoc igitur sit initium piae venerabilium monasteriorum aedificationis."[13]

The procedure inaugurated by the Fourth Ecumenical Council, held at Chalcedon, continued thus to the thirteenth century. From the mass of material in evidence, from the testimony of the various sources viewed above one must conclude that during all this time the bishop's consent was needed for the licit construction of any monastery and the foundation of any religious institute, and also that his consent alone sufficed to make it lawful without the necessity of applying to a higher power.

[10] Can. 10, C. 18, q. 2. The Glossatory here in a parallel passage says this was declared by the Council of Chalcedon. This is one of the two places where any punishment is decreed for a person attempting to found a religious institute without the consent of the proper authority. It is difficult to determine whether Gratian borrowed this from some particular council or whether he inserted it on his own authority. His book in itself has no legal value.

[11] Can. 11, C. 18, q. 2.

[12] This was a revision of the Justinian Code and other laws of the Eastern Empire and was compiled from 906-911. It was the civil law book for the East until the fall of Constantinople in 1453. Cf. Joseph I. Kelly, "Roman Law," *Cath. Encyc.*, IX, 88.

[13] Basilica, Tom. I, L. IV, tit. 1.

Article III

From The IV Lateran Council (1215) to The Council of Trent

The second period in this history begins with the IV Lateran Council held in 1215. For some odd years before this a new order of things regarding monasteries had begun to take shape. Up to the rise of Cluny (910), the monasteries had been entirely independent of each other. The Orders of St. Basil and Benedict were indeed considered as units before this but that was more or less for convenience sake since the individual monasteries acknowledged the same founder and the same rule.[74] The community began in a certain monastery and as a general rule remained there, at least in a certain sense. Thus directly it did not affect the entire Church.[75] The individual houses submitted to no religious superior outside of their own walls, thereby forming a separate entity which can properly be called *sui juris*. It was at Cluny and Citeaux that a change, which was a result of the spirit of reform so badly needed at the time, took place. From these places as from a center emanated a great reform which influenced hundreds of monasteries.[76] These reforms resulted in a departure from many a precedent, chief among which was a highly centralized form of government entirely foreign to Benedictine tradition.[77]

Later on the idea received great impetus from the medicant orders, to which we especially owe the prevailing division into provinces.[78] Monasteries were not only to be of local interest but were to be part of a grand unit; and thus, as these institutes were to be spread over many dioceses it was expedient that a power stronger than that of the local bishop should

[74] Suarez, *De Rel.*, III, L. 2, c. 15, n. 17; Vicente, *Instituta Recentia*, n. 5, p. 4.

[75] Suarez, *De Rel.*, III, L. II, c. 15, n. 17.

[76] Funk, *Manual of Church History*, I, 299.

[77] Cyprian Alston, "Cluny," *Cath. Encyc.* IV, 73.

[78] Wernz, *Jus Decretalium*, III, n. 613: "In Capitulo generali anno 1217 celebrato universus ordo S. Francisci in duodecim provincias cum suis ministris provincialibus fuit distributus."

regulate the establishment of these religious institutes. It is highly probable that this form of union manifest at this period had something to do with the subsequent decree of Innocent III, but, as will soon be seen, he does not adduce this as a reason.

And now a new era in the history of ecclesiastical approbation of religious societies begins. Innocent III, fearing that under the bishops' protection too many new religious communities were being formed, gave forth his well known decree in the IV Lateran Council (1215) whereby he reserved the right of approbation directly to the Holy See. This law given in the thirteenth chapter is entitled, "De novis religionibus prohibitis" and is worded in this manner,

> Ne nimia religionum diversitas gravem in Ecclesia Dei confusionem inducat, firmiter prohibemus ne quis de cetero novam religionem inveniat; sed quicumque voluerit ad religionem converti, unam de approbatis assumat. Similiter qui voluerit religiosam domum fundare de novo, regulam et institutionem accipiat de religionibus approbatis.[79]

An investigation into its historical background will aid us immensely to understand the immediate causes for this new law. The period under consideration is outstanding for its innumerable activities and for its exceptionally large number of heretical movements. Heresies of every description arose, some being merely a renewal of old and forgotten systems, while others were apparently altogether new. Almost invariably the heresies were a reaction to the laxity of the times. The tendency of the age to neglect interior religion and to make it a matter of outward form alone not unnaturally caused a turn in favor of inward religion which frequently took an heretical form.[80]

Principal and outstanding among these are the Albigensians and Waldensians, but it is the latter sect that chiefly

---

[79] Mansi, XXII, 1002.
[80] Funk, *Manual of Church History,* I, 350.

concerns us here. The founder was a certain (Peter?) Waldo.[81] Deeply moved by the passage in the Gospel where our Lord invites the young man to leave all and follow Him[82] and having become acquainted with the story of St. Alexius, he sold all he had, gave away his great fortune, and began his mission of penance.[83] The mode of life was very rigorous and peculiar but, because they professed many errors, he and his followers were soon condemned by Lucius III (1184) and later by his successor, Alexander III.[84] As usual with sects of that sort, they combined the greatest rigorism in some points with the utmost laxity in others. Despite the severe condemnation of these Popes these heretics continued and also established a superstitious mode of life, trying to introduce it as the religious state.[85] In the time of Innocent they, demanding approbation, approached the Holy See. It is no wonder then that Innocent III saw the need of a stronger power than that of the bishops to regulate and guide souls in this higher form of life in the Church. Historians who treat this matter explicitly are in agreement that the immediate cause of this law was the boldness and insistence of this heretical sect.[86]

---

[81] Albers, *Storia Ecclesiastica,* p. 76; De Montor, *The Lives and Times of the Popes,* III, 118, who says, if not the founder, Waldo, was at least the most active promoter of the sect. The system was similar to the Manicheans.

[82] Matth. xix, 16-29.

[83] Albers, *Storia Ecclesiastica,* p. 76.

[84] Bellarminus, L. II, *De Monachis,* c. 4.

[85] Suarez, *De Rel.,* III, L. II, c. 15, n. 15, who refers to the Abbot of Ursberg, who wrote his chronicles in 1212, as the source of his information. The chief errors of the sect, were the rejection of purgatory and intercession for the dead, the denial of oaths, indulgences and the abolition of military service and the death penalty. They were perverse imitators of another kind of poor of that time who were distinguished for their virtues. Cf. Balmes, *European Civilization,* p. 252. It seems in many cases they formed associations of workers, both men and women. The sombre habit which they adopted and their unassuming manners caused them to be called *Humiliati* by the people. The bishops wanted all condemned. But for those who obeyed his injunction, Innocent III (1199) drew up a rule, based on that of St. Augustine, and imposed it upon them. Cf. Mann, *Lives of the Popes* III, 273-274.

[86] Bellarminus, L. II, *De Monachis,* c. 4; Suarez, *De Relig.* III, L. II, c. 15, n. 15.

This reason, however, is not given by Pope Innocent. The reason he gives in the beginning of the canon is, "Ne nimia religionum diversitas gravem in Ecclesia Dei confusionem inducat." Thereby he expresses the fear that the unprecedented multiplication of religious institutes in the previous century or two might bring confusion to the minds of the people and disorder into society. Practically up to this time the Benedictine rule and Order had dominated the Western Church, but in the time before Pope Innocent, several new orders had arisen which were entirely diverse in character. The old rules had been tried for centuries and had been found to be very beneficial; with the new ones there was always danger of things objectionable arising or of error being propagated. This is why the Church was so insistent for many centuries that no new rule be originated, forcing new institutes to follow some approved rule.

Another reason which must have had its influence on the Pope was the inability of the individual bishops to prevent the spread of these heretical imitators of religious life. Manifestly the Pope found difficulty in suppressing them once they were established. Serious harm had already been done to the Church. Much difficulty and many evils could have been avoided, if some greater power had curbed and checked the evil in its infancy. Furthermore since heresy was rampant and was beginning to creep into the religious state, the Pope alone was the proper authority to judge and see that no errors crept into the religious life and struck at the very foundations of Christianity.

Before considering the meaning, extent and other points connected with this law it is better to consider the supplementary legislation which followed shortly after. There is no intention to consider any particular councils,[87] that indirectly or directly refer to it since the state of the Church was such that its regulations could be known by all. The decree of the Lateran was incorporated word for word in the Decret-

[87] The Council of Arles (1234) refers to it—Mansi XXIII, 337; The Council of Champiny (1238)—Mansi, XXII, 495, canon 34.

als of Gregory IX (1234).[89] It was in this form that the decree remained part of the law until the present Code superseded it. Still individuals broke the law and in many cases it is barely possible that they did so with the connivance of their bishops. Violations must have been frequent and grave, as the II General Council of Lyons (1274) deemed it necessary to repeat the law, and that more emphatically. In chapter 23 of the first part the substance of Innocent's law is given in these words:

Religionum diversitatem nimiam, ne confusionem induceret, generale concilum consulta prohibitione vetuit. Sed quia non solum importuna petentium inhiatio illarum postmodum multiplicationem extorsit, verum etiam aliquorum praesumptuosa temeritas diversorum ordinum, praecipue mendicantium, quorum nondum approbationis meruere principium effraenatam quasi multitudinem adinvenit, repetita constitutione districtius inhibente, ne aliquis de cetero novum ordinem aut religionem inveniat, vel habitum novae religionis assumat. Cunctas affatim religiones et ordines mendicantes, post dictum concilium adinventos, qui nullam confirmationem Sedis Apostolicae meruerunt, perpetuae prohibitioni subjicimus, et quatenus processerant, revocamus.[90]

The immediate cause of this repetition is, of course, indicated by the canon itself. The growth of the mendicant orders was astounding and many were beginning new communities irrespective of and without due regard for the regulations of the Church. The canon was received into the Decretals of Boniface VIII (1298).[91] This collection of laws did not abrogate the previous collection.[92]

---

[89] C. 9, X, *de religiosis domibus, ut episcopo sint subjectae,* III, 36.

[90] Mansi, XXIV, 96.

[91] C. unic., *de religiosis domibus,* III, 17, in 6°.

[92] Augustine, *Comm. of Canon Law,* I, 40; Vermeersch-Creusen, *Epitome,* I, n. 28; Blat, *op. cit.,* I, p. 35.

Its very name, *Liber Sextus,* shows that it was to be a continuation of the Gregorian Decretals, with the purpose of supplementing them, and only destroying that portion of the previous law when it legislated contrary to it. In this case the subject matter of both laws is identical though the wording is somewhat different. In our considerations and our analysis these two laws will be considered as one, since where they disagree one supplies what the other lacks.

Still the matter was not completely adjusted, as later Popes found reason to complain. Indirectly the *Clementinae* refer to this law.[93] An examination of the texts which refer to the condemnation of the Beguins indicates that they were declared not to be true religious mainly because the vows of obedience and poverty were lacking, these being considered as essential elements. The lack of approbation is also cited as a cumulative argument against them, thereby signifying the necessity of papal approbation. For the following words are found in the *Extravagantes Joannis XXII*:

Sacris canonibus est interdictum, ne aliquis novum ordinem aut religionem inveniat, vel habitum novae religionis assumat, sed quicumque ad religionem venire voluerit, ingrediatur unam de religionibus approbatis. Nonnulli tamen profanae multitudinis viri . . . Fraticelli . . ., Bizochi, sive Beguinae . . . in Italia et Sicilia sunt . . . . Quidam autem eorum dictum habitum et vivendi ritum a quibusdam episcopis seu eorum superioribus vel aliis ecclesiarum praelatis habuisse profitentur, quos nec eis concedere licuit contra forman Concilii Generalis.[94] These several decrees show us how difficult it was to establish the power of the Holy See in this matter. In many cases the delinquents also claimed to have the permission of the bishop or superior, which John XXII said did not belong to them, since a General Council had reserved it to the Pope.

It was not the intention of the Church to prohibit entirely the foundations of new institutes. Pope Innocent III, great statesman that he was, saw that new religious orders at their origin always filled a need and a want of the times and that the future would bring into prominence changes of conditions which could only be properly cared for by some new religious institute. But in the future permission was not to be given indiscriminately but only as this special need was shown. Even before 1215, St. Francis, desirous of beginning his order which afterwards became so renowned, approached Innocent III asking his approbation. Innocent was suspicious of all reform

---

[93] C. I, *de rel. domib.*, III, 9, in Clem.

[94] Cap. unic., *de rel. domib.*, tit. VII, in Extrav. Joan. XXII.

movements of the time, and so in this case.[95] He endeavored to put Francis aside, or to have him join another established order. The insistence of Francis finally prevailed and his order was then verbally approved.[96] Thus also did the Pope delay in approving the Order of St. Dominic, fearing that their preaching would interfere with the power of the bishops;[97] only consenting to and permitting the foundation based on the Augustinian rule.

Still to a great extent the purpose that Innocent had in mind—the avoidance of too many and too diverse institutes—was undoubtedly obtained. Yet even after his time it did not entirely prevent the growth of new institutes. In the subsequent years many new orders arose and in spite of Rome's disinclination to approve these, they nevertheless obtained her solemn approbation.[98] Although these orders were great aids to the papacy in the course of time, still their establishment was not due to papal projects, as some insinuate, but they were the conceptions of individuals aided by higher inspirations to combat the prevalent evils of the times.[99]

---

[95] Cuthbert, *Life of St. Francis of Assisi*, p. 95; Bellarminus, L. II, *de Monach.*, c. 4; Mann, *Lives of the Popes*, XII, 277. Innocent seeing his coarse garb and generally untidy appearance imagined that he had before him another of those fanatical lay teachers who were then disturbing a large part of Europe, and so summarily bade him begone.

[96] Later, at the IV Lateran Council the Pope caused it to be considered as one of the approved rules, though no formal approbation had been given it. Mann, *Lives of the Popes*, XII, 283. Formal approbation was given by Honorius III, in a solemn bull, *"Solet annuere,"* Nov. 29, 1223—*Constitutiones Urbanae Ordinis Minorum Conventualium St. Francisci*, p. 4.

[97] Mann, *op. cit.*, XII, 284.

[98] The Order of St. Dominic was approved by Honorius III in his constitution, *"Religiosam,"* Dec. 22, 1216—*Bull. Rom.*, III, 309. The Carmelites who came from Asia about this time were approved by the same Pope, Jan. 30, 1226, by the Constitution, *"Ut vivendi"*—*Bull Rom.*, III, 415. Shortly after the Hermits of St. Augustine were united in one body and approved by Alexander IV in his constitution, *"Licet,"* of May 2, 1256—*Bull Rom.*, III, 605. These are generally known as the four mendicant orders. Cf. Wernz, *Jus Decretalium*, III, n. 606. Another that arose at that time and received papal confirmation were the Servites of B. M. V., *"Deo grata,"* Mar. 21, 1256—*Bull. Rom.*, III, 633. Cf. also *Bull. Rom.* III, 346. Besides these there were several others. Cf. Vermeersch, *De Rel. Inst. et. Personis*, I, n. 5.

[99] Balmes, *European Civilization*, p. 255.

A comparison of the canon of the Fourth Council of the Lateran with that of the Council of Lyons brings in evidence the fact that the latter repeats the former but also goes farther. For in the Council of Lyons those that had been formed since the year 1215 without papal consent, even if approved by the bishop, were absolutely forbidden and the faithful were prohibited from leading a religious life in these same communities; and whatever effects may have followed their profession these were expressly invalidated by the positive action of the Pope. The law was only for those living in a community, professing the same rule and wearing a special garb distinctive of their calling.[100]

Neither law was retroactive,[101] not changing in the least the status of those founded before 1215. The words, *de cetero*, indicate the law looked only to the future. Gregory X expressly stated that the Carmelites and Augustinians did not come under this prohibition as they had been founded before the law was made.[102] The nature of a law is such that it never extends to what is past unless the law explicitly so declares, which however, is not the case here. Implicity, in fact, it approves those already established[103] in the words, *unam de approbatis assumat.* The law forbade two things, first the foundation of a new order, second, the profession in one that had not been approved.[104] As a consequence, if the commands of the Council were adhered to these unapproved communities were destined to die for lack of new members.

Thus by this law the decree of the Council of Chalcedon was partially abrogated as it still retained its force with respect to the establishment of religious houses. But it was left solely to the Pope to establish and confirm a new religious institute. As a private individual could not establish and con-

[100] Glossa, in cap. unic., *de rel. domib.*, III, 17, in 6°.
[101] Vicente, *Instit. Recentia*, n. 29, p. 14.
[102] Suarez, *De Rel.*, III, L. II, c. 15, n. 1.
[103] Toso, *De Personis*, L. II, Pars II, p. 13.
[104] Suarez, *op. cit.*, III, L. II, c. 16, n. 26; Bouix, *Tractatus de Jure Reg.*, I, 194.

firm a new institute by his own authority before, so after the enactment of this law a bishop or a particular council likewise was incapable of establishing and confirming any new institute. It was necessary that the Pope or an Ecumenical Council, through an express and previous approbation give the new community a legitimate existence.[105] From this time the approbation of a religious community began to be numbered among the greater causes (*causae majores*) which by law and importance were reserved to the Holy See.[106]

Territorially it was obligatory on the entire Church as promulgated by general councils and decretals which were in no wise limited to a certain territory. Even those who wished to start a new community and adopt one of the four approved rules, (of Sts. Basil, Augustine, Benedict and Francis) were included in the scope of this law. The reasons apparently are that, although the rule had been approved, the new mode of living had not been approved; also the fact that the purpose of the law was to avoid the too divergent multiplication of religious; and, finally Innocent III had expressly declared that anyone desirous of leading a religious life should join one of the already existing and approved religions.[107]

The question may rightly be asked, could a religious community be validly founded after these decrees without the knowledge of Rome? Before answering it is necessary to consider the sense in which the words *religious institute* are used. Persons living individually or together in the world and observing one or all of the three evangelical counsels can in the widest sense of the term be said to be true religious. Yet no responsible canonist can deny the ability of the Church to add something to the bare essentials of religious life, without which no true religious institute may be had. With this law then as a basis, canonists of the succeeding years considered

[105] Wernz, *Jus Decretalium*, III, n. 610.

[106] Santi, *Praelectiones Jur. Can.*, III, tit. 31, n. 3, p. 276; Larraona, "Commentarium Codicis", *Comm. pro Rel.*, II (1921), 282, footnote n. 130. Vicente, *Inst. Rec.*, n. 28, p. 13.

[107] Bouix, *De Jure Reg.*, I, 205.

four things as absolutely necessary in order to make a community truly religious. These were: first, the three evangelical counsels; second, these had to be strengthened by perpetual vows; third, the vows had to be taken in a legitimately approved institute; fourth, the members had to live under a certain rule or constitution.[108]

Added to this, it should be noted that in this period solemn vows were invariably taken in all religious institutes. Because some discussion arose whether religious congregations came under this law, their establishment by the bishops will be considered later. Here orders in the strict sense are only being considered. The question is then, whether the Church laid down the law expressing the necessity of approbation with the intention to make such establishments merely illicit or with the intention to make their foundation invalid, so that any approbation, except the Supreme Pontiff's, would not suffice to found an order. Viewing it is in this light canonists generally agree that it was an irritating or invalidating law.[109]

The context of the law itself does not lead one to that conclusion, rather, taking the words as they stand one is led to believe that such an act contrary to the letter of the law was merely illicit. Laws in general are not invalidating unless it is so stated explicitly or implicitly in the law itself. There is no such implication here. Considering only the last words of the II Council of Lyons, *et quatenus processerant revocamus*, one would be inclined to the belief that a positive act of the Council was used in this case to make invalid the illicit foundations mentioned. But a special revocation may have been necessary or thought useful because of the many incidental

[108] Schmalzgrueber, *Jus. Eccles.*, Lib. III, tit. 31, n. 13; Wernz, *Jus Decretalium*, III, n. 590: "Quare ad essentiam status religiosi partim ex natura rei, iureque divino, partim ex iure ecclesiastico nunc vigente quatuor requiruntur."

[109] Bouix, *De Jure Reg.*, I, 198; Suarez, *De Rel.*, III, L. II, c. 16, n. 9; also c. 15, n. 1; Angel a SS. Corde, *Praelectiones Juris Canonici*, II, L. III, t. 31, p. 81; Mocchegiani, *Jurisprudentia Ecclesiastica*, n. 17, p. 16; Bellarminus, L. II, *de Monachis*, c. 4; Schmalzgrueber, *Jus Eccles.*, Lib. III, tit. 31, n. 22. q. 5.

effects and consequences which would flow from such invalidation. In the case of these unapproved institutes the Pope may have thought it necessary to revoke them publicly so as to leave no room for doubt. Or these words may have been added to give strength to the decree. Since the text does not help to make clear the point regarding validity, authors have recourse to arguments drawn from the nature of the religious state, and from related passages of the Decretals.

The religious state, in itself, is the state of prefection since that is its nature and without this state of perfection as the main objective it could not exist. However, it seems absurd to say that a state of perfection can be found in a state of life which is expressly forbidden, or against the will of the Supreme Pontiff. Besides no one can contract in the name of God and accept the offering made to God unless he has received that power from God Himself. No one has received this power except the Pope, and so it is necessary that the manner of contracting and establishing such a state, at least in as far as it pertains to the one accepting and in whose hands the vows are made, should be instituted by the Church and in some manner approved. This argument is based on the fact that a religious by his profession gives himself to God, which is called *traditio* and which the superior accepts in the name of God. Under these circumstances the *traditio* could not properly be made as the superior had no authority and besides it seems unreasonable that God should accept one in a prohibited state.[110]

The affirmative opinion regarding the invalidity of contrary acts is strengthened by the *Clementinae*, in the passage already mentioned, where one of the reasons given to prove that the Beguins were not true religious was the lack of approbation by the Church authorities.[111] Also in the Decretals of Boniface VIII it is mentioned explicitly that only that profession was valid which was made in an institute approved

[110] Bouix, *De Reg.*, I, 199; Angel a. SS. Corde, *Praelectiones Iuris Can.*, II, p. 81.

[111] C. 1, *de rel. domib.*, III, 9, in Clem.

by the Holy See.[112] Likewise in the *Extravagantes* of John XXII married persons are permitted to enter an approved religion,[113] and the Glossa had here that to enter any other would not have been of any value since others are entirely forbidden and recalled.[114] Bouix is of the opinion that the text of the law itself evidently declares these illicit establishments invalid.[115]

The consensus of writers here is well nigh unanimous and Suarez infers that Cajetan was the only one inclined to the contrary opinion.[116] Added to this is the unbroken tradition and the witness of writers from the thirteenth century to the present who all affirm that the Apostolic See alone has the power to create an order or a religion in the strict sense of the term. The extension of this law to religion congregations will be discussed fully when we come to treat of these in the next chapter.

As to the history of the observance of this law in the following centuries down to the time of the Council of Trent the conclusion is forced upon us that in the main it was generally observed.[117] Later Popes apparently found little need to repeat this legislation and history shows that the power of the Holy See was constantly being recognized here, as a glance at the many institutes which came before it for approbation aptly demonstrates. The last public utterance seems to have been the case of the Beguins.[118] Whether the Popes interfered publicly like this in other cases that were called to their attention we do not know. It is somewhat probable that in the general demoralization and deterioration so noticeable before the Protestant revolution many violations may have occurred, but history does not substantiate us in the belief that a general nonobservance of the law prevailed.

---

[112] Cap. unic., *de Voto,* in 6°.

[113] C. unic., *de voto et voti redemptione,* tit. VI, in Extrav. Joan XXII.

[114] Glossa in C. unic., *de voto et voti redemptione,* tit. VI., in Extrav. Joan XXII.

[115] Bouix, *De Jure Reg.*, I. 201.

[116] Suarez, *De Rel.* III, L. II, c. 16, n. 4.

[117] Verhoefen, *Examen Historicum et Canonicum,* I, c. 4, n. 11.

[118] C. 1, *de rel. domib.*, III, 11, in Clem.

CHAPTER II

ARTICLE I

The Growth of Religious Congregations

The Church's answer to the challenge brought out by the Protestant upheaval had been given in the Council of Trent (1545-1563). Crying abuses had called for correction for years and the warning had gone unheeded to the subsequent disunion of Christendom. It was not in the least surprising that the religious orders of the times imbibed the poisonous spirit of decay and suffered themselves to depart from their pristine rigor and high ideals. Not all, it must be said in truth, were corrupt; but there were many who were contaminated by the contagion of the world and the general decadence of faith and morals so characteristic of the age.

What more becoming then, seeing that religious communities had fallen from their high state, that the Council should endeavor to restore and put new life into them to the end that they should once more be the choicest adornment of Mother Church? The twenty-fifth session of this Council is devoted exclusively to the reformation of religious. The question however that primarily concerns us, the proper ecclesiastical approbation for religious institutions, did not enter under discussion, at least it is not recorded in any of the Council's many decrees. The desire was not so much for new laws as for enforcement of the old. Its purpose was the restoration of the old and regular discipline where it had fallen, the preservation of the same where it had been conserved and the observance of the three vows according to the rule professed.[1] These constituted its main objectives and were the basis of that salutary legislation the effects of which have lasted to our days.

Let it be repeated, the Council of Trent does not refer directly to our subject. And yet indirectly this Council concerns us very much since it inaugurated a reform and promulgated certain laws which were to be the basis of new decrees, or rather of a restatement of old laws shortly after by Pope Pius V. In chapter one it prescribed: "Regulares omnes ad regulam, quam professi sunt, praescriptam vitam instituant; id ut fiat superiores sedulo curent." The return to the ancient discipline was all the Council sought as the remedy to cure the evils to which the monasteries had succumbed.

But it is in chapter five that the cloister of nuns is treated and the law laid down which was to be the source of unending discussion and which was to be often disregarded. It was expressed in these words:

Bonifacii VIII constitutionem, quae incipit, *Periculoso*, renovans sancta synodus, universis episcopis sub obtestatione divini judicii et interminatione maledictionis aeternae praecipit, ut in omnibus monasteriis sibi subjectis ordinaria, in aliis vero sedis apostolicae auctoritate, clausuram sanctimonialium, ubi violata fuerit, diligenter restitui, et ubi inviolata est, conservari maxime procurent . . . .Nemini autem sanctimonialium liceat post professionem exire a monasterio. . . .Ingredi autem septa monasterii nemini liceat.[2]

The law of Boniface VIII was once more to be enforced, as it seems to have fallen into desuetude for some time before this. His decree was, "Sancimus, universas et singulas moniales presentes atque futuras, cujuscumque religionis sint vel ordinis, in quibuslibet mundi partibus existentes, sub perpetua in suis monasteriis debere de cetero permanere clausura.[3]

[1] Sess. XXV, *De Regularibus*, c. 1.
[2] Sess. XXV, *De Regularibus*, c. 5.
[3] C. un., *De Regularibus et Monial.*, III, 16, in. 6°.

The effect of the enforcement of the laws would have been to force all members of communities of sisters to give up all contact with the world. The law of the cloister in general prohibits the ingress of women into the monasteries of men and the entrance of persons of both sexes into those of sisters.[4] Besides it strictly forbids to religious women egress outside of the monastery walls except under the most urgent reasons. Though of ecclesiastical origin and thus not essential to the religious state,[5] it had been rigorously enforced for many centuries and the Council was anxious that this good custom continue. The evident purpose was to segregate the nuns especially from the companionship of men, that they might have more time for prayer and that their minds might solely tend toward God.[6]

For many years before the Council a gradual evolution of the interior constitution of religious institutes had come about. The aim of the Council was to check this. For despite the prohibition of Boniface VIII, referred to above, certain communities arose without the consent of Rome, though not without her knowledge, and these did not observe the cloister and had no provision for it in their rule. Some of the older communities that were obliged to the cloister also had dropped its observance that they might adopt the spirit of the times. Besides some of the new communities broke another traditional regulation of the Church in assuming only simple vows. Those that had their origin through the bishops, as some did, could only take simple vows, for though solemn vows owe their origin to custom and positive legislation of the Church, still a decretal of Boniface VIII declares: "Illud solum votum debere dici solemne quod solemnisatum fuerit. . .per professionem expressam vel tacitam, factum alicui de religionibus per sedem apostolicam approbatis."[7]

---

[4] Ojetti, *Synopsis Rerum Moralium*, I, n. 1162.
[5] Wernz, *Jus Decret.*, III, n. 591.
[6] Benedict XIV, *De Synodo Dioecesana*, I, L. IX, c. 15, n. 7.
[7] C. un., *de voto*, III, 15, in 6°.

So then, the bishop's approbation did not suffice to make the vows solemn, nor could it be said that the Popes at any time tolerated a custom contrary to this law, though the Pontiffs preceding the Council must have been cognizant of the things that were going on. This much is certain that the Holy See from the time of Innocent III to the Council of Trent did not approve any but religious with solemn vows,[8] at least that was the universal and general practice.

The Council of Trent thus forms a landmark in the history of religious orders, as through its decrees they were enabled to arise from the low state of decadence into which they had fallen.[9] The shining exceptions that shone out so well amidst the corruption cannot disguise the fact that decadence had set in. Testimony to corroborate this low ebb of monastic life is shown in this that in the succeeding century all the orders underwent a reform. No one was more influential in this reform movement than Pius V (1565-1572), who was elevated to the papacy but two years after the Council of Trent. His was the era of reform, for to him was given the task of enforcing the decrees of the Council, and history speaks well of the manner in which he performed this difficult undertaking. He corrected abuses on all sides within the church and in all he did he was animated solely by the purpose of upholding faith and discipline.

It is his attitude toward religious institutes that concerns us here. Like the Council he saw that the preservation of monasticism and the guarantee of new life was not to be found in novelties and new modes of life but rather in a return to the manner of life traced out for these by their saintly founders.[10] Animated with this spirit he inaugurated reforms on all sides. His reforming activities were so many and various that we can only wonder that he could have accomplished so much in so short a time. In determination and zeal he excelled all other

[8] Angel, de S. S. Corde, *Prael. Jur .Can.*, III, 276.
[9] Pastor, *History of the Popes*, XVII, 240.
[10] Pastor, *History of the Popes*, XVII, 263.

popes of his age, and it was characteristic of him that he was never satisfied with what he had done.[11]

Strictly speaking the third period of our history should begin with him but because his work was done under the shadow and influence of the Council of Trent it is better to commence this part of our history with the Council. One thing peculiarly noticeable about Pius in his relation to monastic institutes is the individual character of most of his decrees. In his opinion there were plenty of general laws; and so, as a rule, his laws were of a more particular nature, he having particular institutes in mind. As he noticed abuses or failure to observe the laws of the Council he wrote letters urging the strictest and most exact observance. And so many of his letters were addressed to particular orders when evils or deviations from the law came to his notice.[12] Communities refusing to heed his warning were suppressed entirely.[13]

Two of his constitutions with regard to religious are outstanding; the one "*Circa pastoralis*" of May 29, 1566, which certainly had universal application;[14] the other, "*Lubricum vitae*"[15] of November 17, 1568, which is thought by some to be also general in extent. The former considered only women communities, while the latter had application to men. Neither had any direct reference to the necessity of approbation by the Church for the beginning of new institutes. Both express certain requirements which are to be present in all religious establishments, which if they were absent would cause the Church to disapprove that life. The power of these decrees, especially that for women, was to be felt for over three hundred years in the founding of new institutions. For therein a policy

[11] Pastor, *History of the Popes*, XVII, 286.

[12] Cf. *Bull. Rom.*, VII, 666, 676, 679, 691, 813, 821, etc.

[13] For an example cf. *Bull. Rom.* VII. 888. The Humiliati were also suppressed. Pastor, *op. cit.*, XVII, 244. In Spain many of the laxer religious were suppressed, especially many branches of the third order. Pastor, *op. cit.*, XVII, 252, 258.

[14] Fontes, 112.

[15] *Bull. Romanum*, VII, 725.

was formed from which the Holy See found it difficult to recede, yet even more difficult to enforce, which was only changed by force of necessity and custom.

But to return to the constitution, "*Circa pastoralis.*" The salient points of the constitution are contained in the following paragraphs:

I. Hac igitur perpetuo valitura Constitutione, inhaerentes Constitutioni fel. rec. Bonifacii Papae VIII Praedecessoris nostri, quae incipit *Periculoso,*[10] et decretis Concilii Tridentini[11] super clausura Monialium editis, auctoritate Apostolica tenore praesentium statuimus, atque perpetuo decernimus, universas, et singulas Moniales, praesentes atque futuras cujuscumque Religionis, Ordinis, vel militarium, etiam Hierosolymitarum sint, quae vel iam receptae sint, vel in posterum in quibusvis Monasteriis, sive domibus recipientur, et tacite vel expresse religionem professae, etiam si conversae, aut quocumque alio nomine appellentur, etiam si ex institutis, vel fundationibus earum regulae ad claururam non teneantur, nec unquam in earum Monasteriis, seu domibus, etiam ab immemorabili tempore ea servata non fuerit, sub perpetua in suis Monasteriis seu domibus debere de cetero permanere clausura, juxta formam dictae Constitutionis fel. rec. Bonifacii Papae VIII Praedecessoris nostri, quae incipit *Periculoso,* in sacro Concilio Tridentino approbatam, et innovatam, quam Nos Auctoritate praefata etiam approbamus, et innovamus, in omnibus, et per omnia, ac illam districte observari mandamus.

II. Quod si aliquae Moniales forsan reperiantur, quae consuetudine etiam immemorabili, aut instituto, vel fundatione regulae suae fretae animo obstinato huic clausurae resistant, aut quoquomodo reluctentur, Ordinarii una cum Superioribus earum, omnibus juris, et facti remediis compellant easdem tamquam rebelles, et incorrigibiles ad praecise subeundam dictam calusuram, perpetuo observandam.

III. Mulieres quoque quae Tertiariae, seu de Poenitentia dicuntur cujuscumque fuerint Ordinis in congregatione viven-

[10] C. unic., *De Statu regularium,* III, 16, in 6°.
[11] Sess. XXV, *De Regularibus,* c. 5.

tes, si et ipsae professae fuerint, ita ut solemne votum emiserint, ad clausuram praecise, ut praemittitur, et ipsae teneantur; quod si votum solemne non emiserint, Ordinarii una cum Superioribus earum hortentur, et persuadere studeant, ut illud emittant, et profiteantur, ac post emissionem, et professionem eidem clausurae se subiiciant; quod si recusaverint, et aliquae ex eis inventae fuerint scandalose vivere, severissime puniantur.

IV. Ceteris autem omnibus sic absque emissione professionis, et clausura vivere valentibus interdicimus, et perpetuo prohibemus, ne in futurum ullam aliam prorsus in suum Ordinem, Religionem, Congregationemque recipiant. Quod si contra hujusmodi hanc nostram prohibitionem, et decretum aliquas receperint, eas ad sic vivendum omnino inhabiles reddimus, ac illarum quaslibet professiones, et receptiones irritas facimus, et annullamus.

The rest of the ten chapters consider the means of sustenance for these cloistered nuns, and also direct the Ordinaries and others in power to publish this decree and see to its enforcement. The civil authorities were also requested to help. The ninth paragraph annuls and revokes all previous contrary customs, indults, privileges and the like.

In this constitution, Pius V shows his endeavors to live up to the entire spirit of the Council of Trent. The words of paragraph one show the law was only for communities of women. The wording of the law is very precise. Even those who had not been obliged to the cloister by their vows or constitutions are commanded to observe it. Tertiaries living a common life also were to take solemn vows. Clearly this was for all those women who were living in a community and wore a garb distinct from that of the world; those tertiaries living in their own homes were not affected in the least by this constitution.[13]

---

[13] Bouix, *De Jure Reg.*, I, 323.

The invalidating conditions of paragraph four render a woman incapable of becoming a religious unless the obligation of the cloister was assumed. The words of the law force one to the conclusion that solemn vows must be taken under pain of invalidity; and it is well known that the mind of Pope Pius was that all should take solemn vows. Henceforth, due partly to this law and partly to custom, solemn vows and the cloister were so intimately connected that the obligation of the cloister was a necessary consequence of solemn profession,[19] so that the direct exclusion by the will of the obligation of the cloister invalidated any profession in the eyes of the Church.[20] The law of the IV Council of the Lateran was still in force, and so it was reserved to the Holy See alone to approve any new religious community; but after this decree before the Apostolic See would approve any new community the new institute would have to embrace the stated conditions.

While the constitution *Circa pastoralis* is clear, the other, *Lubricum vitae*, which is sometimes said to apply to men is not so evident, at least as far as its extent is concerned. But before reviewing its provisions it is well for us to know its contents. The title given by the compiler of the *Bullarium Romanum* is this:

De solemni trium votorum substantialium professione regulari emittenda, et una ex Regulis approbatis eligenda ab omnibus, qui in diversis congregationibus et domibus, sub voluntaria obedientia et extra solemne votum Religionis, vivant, et habitum a saecularibus presbyteris distinctum deferunt.[21]

The chapters of interest in this treatise have this to say:

I. Itaque. . . statuimus ut omnes et singuli priores, praepositi et alii praesidentes generales, provinciales et conventuales, necnon canonici et fratres Sancti Georgii in Alga Venetarium ac Eremitarum Sancti Hieronymi, alias Beati Petri

[19] Disceptatio synoptica ex S. Cong. E. E. & Reg.—*A. S. S.*, IX, 158.
[20] *A. S. S.*, IX, 158.
[21] *Bull. Rom.*, VII, 725; Nov. 17, 1568.

Pisarum, et omnium a quarumcumque aliarum congregationum necnon ecclesiarum, domorum et conventuum, in communi et sub obedientia voluntaria et extra votum solemne Religionis viventes, quorum habitus a saecularibus presbyteris est distinctus, qui Religionem amplecti et professionem regularem solemnem emittere voluerint, id in suis quisque conventibus et domibus, intra viginti quatuor horarum spatium. . . .palam et sponte deliberent et declarent, inde convocato quamprimum, per singulas hujusmodi congregationes, generali vel alio supremo, juxta morem cujusque congregationis, capitulo, ibique electa una, sub qua degant, ex Regulis approbatis, in quam major pars vocum ipsius capituli consenseri, trium votorum substantialium professionem regularem intra mensem solemniter emittant. . . .

III. Non obstantibus fundationibus et institutionibus ac statutis et consuetudinibus congregationum. . . .juramento, confirmatione apostolica vel quavis firmitate alia roboratis; privilegiis quoque, exemptionibus et indultis apostolicis, etc.

V. Ac etiam volumus quod ipsarum praesentium exempla, etiam impressa, et praelati ecclesiastici vel eius curiae sigillo et notarii publici manu obsignata, eamdem illam fidem ubique locorum, in indicio et extra illud, faciant, quam ipsae praesentes facerent, si ibi ostenderentur aut exhiberentur.

Paragraph two deals with the punishments to be meted out to those refusing to obey within the time determined by law; and commands the superiors and others to see to the enforcement under the threat of deprivation from office, dignities and beneficies; and adds besides the threat of excommunication.

The contents show that it was a general law as in paragraph four it is so promulgated. It included all communities where common life prevailed, where a distinctive garb was worn as a sign of voluntary obedience. So that after this decree all those communities with only simple vows were obliged to take solemn vows, as the words, "et omnium, a quarumcumque aliarum congregationum" hardly leave any reason for doubting this extension. Bizzarri holds that it was obligatory on all communities of men,[22] while others again hold that it probably was not.[23] Addressed chiefly to the Canons of St. George[24] and the Hermits of St. Jerome, still it included all the congregations of the time. Since it made no distinct reference to future ones, these were not to be obliged by force of this decree to profess solemn vows. Besides the threat of invalidity of profession is not given here as in the constitution "*Circa pastoralis,*" nor is reference made to any future professions in new institutes.

It is known with certitude what the mind of Pope Pius V was, but the mind of the lawgiver is not the law and here an extension beyond the context can not be justified. Pius saw fit to apply what had been the law up to his time though it was mainly based on custom. That he desired to enforce it in all communities of men in the future is likewise very clear; for through his life he did not look with favor upon any community with simple vows. This is shown by his many letters but more so by his attempts to change the constitution of the Society of Jesus.[25]

When St. Ignatius and his first companions formed the Society of Jesus with solemn vows they had as one of their chief aims the maintaining of their high standard of learning. It was thus their intention that only those would be admitted to membership who had proved themselves learned.[26] There

[22] Bizzarri, *Collectanea,* p. 743, footnote.

[23] Vicente, *Instit. Rec.,* n. 54, p. 27; Larraona, "Commentarium Codicis—*Comm. pro. Rel.,* I (1920), 48.

[24] This is shown also by two decrees published later. "*Ex incumbente,*" Sept. 11, 1569—Bull. Rom., VII, 772. Paragraph one of this decree mentions that the congregation of St. George received the bull, "*Lubricum vitae,*" and chose the rule of St. Augustine and professed solemn vows. Then in a *Motu Proprio* of May 22, 1571—Bull. Rom., VII, 915 Pius tells us that these same canons obeyed his decree and made regular profession; as a reward he gives them special precedence. An account of the origin of these Canons of St. George is found in *Bull. Rom.* IV, 645. From this it is seen that they were organized by the local Ordinary with the permission of Boniface IX. According to A. Allaria, "Canons Regular"—*Cath. Encyc.,* III, 296, they were founded at Venice in 1404.

[25] Pastor, *History of the Popes,* XVII, 278.

[26] Pastor, *History of the Popes,* XVII, 279.

was to precede a long term or period of trial before one was eligible to solemn profession. It is easy to see that their number would have been very small, and so they accepted others as coadjutors. These took only simple vows and remained in these for many years. If a person were unsuited for the purpose of the Society, the general could dispense from the simple vows and dismiss him. Paul III and Julius III had approved this practice. Pius V, however, was not satisfied and demanded an explanation for these simple vows of the scholastics. For a time the Society's reason sufficed[27], but a new blow was struck by another decree which required solemn vows before ordination in any religious institute.[28] The Jesuits complained and after much discussion the Pope heeded the complaint, though obliging them to support any priest dispensed from his simple vows.[29] This attitude towards the Jesuits clears all doubts as to the mind of Pius regarding solemn profession for all religious. It also seems to show that Pius endeavored to solve each case that was brought before him in its own light, which accounts for his many particular laws.

This attitude did animate the Holy See in later years to the extent that it was desirous that all new religious institutes profess solemn vows, so that to some degree it was not favorably disposed towards those with only simple vows. Shortly after the death of Pius V some communities were approved by Rome. These had no intention to profess solemn vows, yet there was no direct limitation placed on Rome's approval. The Holy See desired that all take solemn vows but did not insist to the extent of denying approbation to those which would not receive them.

---

[27] Pastor, *op. cit., XVII*, 280.

[28] *"Romanus Pontifex,"* Oct. 14, 1568—*Bull. Rom.*, VII, 723. This extended the decree of the Council of Trent for secular clergy to the Canons Regular and was to prevent a priest's not being ascribed to any diocese or religious community.

[29] Pastor, *op. cit.*, XVII, 280.

History thus teaches that the regulations of Pius V were not so strictly and strenuously enforced against men as against women. One would think, that even if, as some claim, the constitution, "*Lubricum vitae*," did not apply to all men communities, still the Holy See would follow Pius' most evident purpose. But not many years later many congregations of men were publicly confirmed by Rome.[30] Some of these, it is true, later on became Orders, but there were others among them which always retained their character as congregations with simple vows. So many approbations lead to the conclusion that if any law did exist it was soon nullified by constant approbation contrary to it.

But the case with congregations of women is totally different. For a long time the succeding Popes sought to apply the laws of Pius V, forcing all to profess solemn vows and to observe the cloister. It was only gradually and only after a long period of time that congregations of women were acknowledged by Rome. The history of their recognition by the Church may be summed up briefly in this manner; at first forbidden and opposed, then tolerated, later praised, and only after more than two centuries were they formally approved by Rome.[31]

Even though the constitution of Pius V mentions only Tertiaries, authors are in accord in saying that all congregations

[30] Some for example are: the Clerics Regular for administering to the sick, *Ex omnibus*, Sixtus V, March 18, 1586—*Bull. Rom.*, VIII, 669; the Poor Clerics of the Mother of God of Pious Schools, Paul V, *Ad ea*, March 6, 1617—*Bull. Rom.* XII, 382; the Clerics Regular of the Mother of God, *Ex quo divina*, Clement VIII, October 13, 1595—*Bull. Rom.*, X, 227; the Doctrinarians, *Exposcit debitum*, Clement VIII, December 23, 1597—*Bull. Rom.*, X, 411; the Congregation of the Missions, *Ex commissa*, Alexander VII, September 22, 1655—*Bull. Rom.*, XVI, 67; the Congregation of the Bethlemites, *Ecclesiae catholicae*, Innocent XI, March 29, 1687—*Bull. Rom.*, XIX, 735; the Passionists, *Supremi apostolatus*, Clement XIV, December 16, 1769—*Bull. Romani Continuatio*, VII, 73; the Congregation of the Holy Redeemer, *Ad pastoralis*, Benedict XIV, February 25, 1749. Cf. Jos. Wuest, *Redemptorists—Cath. Encyc.*, XII, 683.

[31] Larraona, *Comm. pro Rel.*, I (1920), 46.

were thereby included and thus forbidden to exist.[32] After that time no congregation could licitly exist,[33] much less enjoy any ecclesiastical rights. Furthermore in paragraph three of the constitution "*Circa pastoralis*," the Pope declares that such congregations are incapable of receiving new members, nor can the latter validly be admitted to profession, and it seems that this inability extended also to congregations of the future. Hence those existing were left the alternative either of making solemn profession and adopting the enclosure or of dying a slow but sure death from their incapability of receiving new members.

But the issue was not dead, nor was it settled by any means. It lay dormant for a time, but rose in time to be a puzzle and difficulty for both legislator and canonist. Despite the solemn condemnation of Pius his decrees never fully obtained their desired effect, viz., the total abolition of congregations of women and the observance of the strict cloister.[34] Many of the old congregations apparently continued in existence after his death, and new ones sprang up in the course of years. In practically all cases no papal approval was obtained.

Subsequent popes did not issue any new prohibitions or repeat the old ones within the next hundred years. They surely must have been acquainted with the state of affairs, yet they remained silent. It seems they either feared greater evils would result from their attempts to suppress them or thought the law too severe and unenforceable. Or their purpose may have been not to do anything, excepting as the evils arose which Pius feared thus forcing them to act. Then again they may have realized the good done by these new communities in the form of charity, for the communities which arose in the seventeenth

[32] Bouix, *De Jure Reg.*, I, 219; Larraona, "Commentarium codicis"—*Comm. pro Rel.*, I (1920), 47; Vermeersch, *De Rel.*, I, n. 8, p. 49; Lucidi, *De Visitatione Sac. Liminum*, II, n. 263.

[33] Wernz, *Jus Decret.*, III, n. 608.

[34] Lucidi, *De Visitatione Sac. Liminum*, II, n. 264; Larraona, *Comm. pro Rel.*, I (1920), Januensis, *Thesaurus Resol.*, T. XVIII, p. 28, as quoted by Bouix, *De Jure Reg.*, I, 326.

and eighteenth centuries were most remarkable for their practical character.[35]

The first papal reference to them came in 1667. In his Constitution "*Alias propositas,*" Dec. 10, 1667,[36] Clement IX approved certain decisions made by the Congregation of Bishops and Regulars to various questions proposed for solution. The doubts had reference to the women of a certain conservatory. These women lived together with simple vows, and wore the habit of St. Dominic. The questions proposed are of little concern here. They were practical, about the right to wear certain things over their garb, about the age of admission, the establishment of a chapel, and other similar points. A response was given and besides certain favors were granted to them. There is no word of approbation in these concessions, still it could not have been unknown to the Pope that they were not living in accordance with the law of Pius V.

But another Pope shortly afterwards was more outspoken. This was Benedict XIII, who even went so far as to say that he did not wish to prohibit Tertiaries with simple vows, thus implicitly approving them.[37] The tenor of his bull is to confer various privileges on the Dominican Order; and as a mark of favor also on various Tertiaries under their charge. In paragraph 38 he writes:

Tertiariis praedictis emisso solo castitatis voto collegialiter viventibus haud prohibemus, immo exoptamus in Domino, suaderi trium votorum etiam solemnium emissionem, ipsamque clausuram, juxta propositum Constit. VIII, S. Pii V incipientis *Circa pastoralis.* Inhaerents tamen litteris apostolicis superius memoratis Julii II, in quibus tertiariis S. Dominici collegialiter permittitur emittere tria vota, declaraturque per haec ipsa ad clausuram minime teneri, aut ad officium divinum, magis quam et regulam tertii habitus, ac aliis Clem. IX *Alias*

[35] Funk, *Manual of Church History,* II, 171.
[36] *Bull. Rom.,* XVII, 609-610.
[37] Bull., "*Pretiosus,*" of May 25, 1727.—*Bull. Rom.,* XXII, 522-542.

propositis, X dec. 1667, in quibus tertiariae collegialiter viventes ad clausuram nullatenus compelluntur; attendents insuper per annos, ut accepimus, centum et sexaginta ab edita dicta constitutione S. Pii V, et per saeculum et ultra post decretum Congregationis E. E. et Reg. emanatum 20 dec. 1616, eiuscemodi tertiariis collegialiter viventes pluribus in locis, scientibus et tacentibus Ordinariis, floruisse, ac etiamnum florere sine clausura, declaramus, volumus et mandamus, easdem ad neutrum absolute teneri aut esse compellendas; non obstantibus contrariis ordinationibus etiam apostolicis, quibus expresse per praesentes derogamus.

In this letter he quotes Julius II and Clement IX as though they likewise had permitted Tertiary congregations to exist. Julius II was Supreme Pontiff (1503-1513) before the Council of Trent and so strictly has no place here. As to Clement IX, there is nothing in his letter to suppose more than mere toleration. This paragraph of the bull of Benedict XIII also shows mere toleration by the Holy See, not approbation.[38] He weakens the force of the law by merely advising these religious to act as Pius V ordered but in no way were they compelled to do so. Historically the document is of great value for it shows that even in 1616, just fifty years after the constitution "*Circa pastoralis*" was put in force, troubles had arisen with congregations not observing the cloister and taking only simple vows. The decree of the Congregation of Bishops and Regulars in 1616 had no effect on stopping this growth, and many were flourishing with the permission of and under the supervision of the Ordinaries.

Yet all this time the law was still in force. The congregations were merely tolerated and left under the jurisdiction of the Ordinary. The toleration that Benedict XIII decreed was only of short duration, as only a few years later, March 31, 1732, his successor, Clement XII, in a bull, "*Romanus Pontifex,*"[39] revoked, together with many other concessions all the

[38] Bouix, *De Jure Reg.*, I, 325.
[39] *Bull. Rom.*, XXIII, 323-327.

privileges and favors granted in the letters mentioned. The bull "*Pretiosus*" is mentioned among these,[40] and the conditions which prevailed before Benedict XIII were again in force.[41] The status of religious congregations at this time is best described by Benedict XIV who is recognized as the greatest canonist of all times. Speaking of the various bodies of Tertiaries [42] that had arisen, he said: "Tamen ut ratio Sanctissimi Pontificis habeatur, et de ipsius Decreti observantia studium ostendatur, Sedes Apostolica Tertiarias ejusmodi dissimulare et tamquam sua auctoritate minime probatas Episcoporum jurisdictione permittere censuerit."[43] Then he refers to a case which happened when he was secretary to the Sacred Congregation of the Council. The Bishop of Luni, Italy, had asked certain questions concerning the Franciscan Tertiaries in his diocese. The answer was given, January 3, 1723, as follows: "Earum monasterium esse subjectum omnimodo jurisdictioni Episcopi, citra tamen approbationem quoad illud."[44]

It did not take him long then, once he became Pope, to clarify the issues in the case and to set aright conditions which must have been well nigh intolerable. Outlawed as these institutions were, proscribed by written law, it was essential that, since many had been permitted to exist, something should be done to give them rights and privileges in the eyes of the law. This Benedict XIV proceeded to do in his constitution, "*Quamvis Justo,*" April 30, 1794.[45] Though directed to one particular institute this constitution was to be the form for all similar cases of religious congregations in their relations to the local Ordinary. Through this constitution religious congregations may be considered as having been granted legitimate and juridical existence.[46] Thus the foundations were laid for their great

[40] Par. I—*Bull. Rom.*, XXIII, 324.

[41] Benedict XIV, *Instit. Eccl.*, 105, n. 79.

[42] One must always remember that he is speaking of Tertiaries who lived in communities and took simple vows.

[43] Benedict XIV, *Inst. Eccl.*, 29, n. 6.

[44] Benedict XIV, *Inst. Eccl.*, 29, n. 6.

[45] *Fontes*, n. 398.

[46] Larraona, *Comm. pro Rel.*, I (1920), 49.

future evolution and the first scheme or plan of the constitutions of religious congregations of women was enunciated.[47]

The immediate cause of this constitution was a dispute between the Ordinary of Augusta and two conservatories of English Ladies in his diocese. In his usual clear manner Benedict XIV gives an account of the origin of the institutes in question, a history of the trouble, and also of the efforts of Mary Ward to establish her institute against the prohibitions of bishops and Roman Pontiffs. He distinguished the English Ladies here from the group that Mary Ward had attempted to start, tracing their history from their exile from England on account of the persecutions raging there to the time of their dispute with the Bishop.[48] He then undertook to define with exactness their ecclesiastical status in the following words:

§ 4. Expositum fuit [Clementi IX], nonnullas et Anglia Catholicas Puellas Nobiles. . .sibi quandam Domum, seu Conservatorium constituisse, ibique vixisse, aliasque subinde Puellas, inter eas postmodum receptas, tunc pariter vivere, ac praeter alia pietatis opera, Puellis, quae ipsis erudiendae tradebantur, docendis et instruendis incumbere. . . . Cumque hujusmodi Regularum revisio antea commissa fuisset Congregationi S. R. E. Cardinalium Tridentini Concilii Interpretum; haec autem, Regulis ipsis mature examinatis, eidem Clementi sententiam suam pro earum approbatione aperuisset; Pontifex ipse, per supradictas Literas Apostolicas, easdem confirmare non dubitavit.

§ 5. Ipsis denique Literis apposita legitur clausula salutaris, videlicet, Caeterum non intendimus per praesentes ipsum Conservatorium in aliquo approbare: quae tunc apponi consuevit, quum approbantur, seu confirmantur Regulae alicujus Conservatorii, aut Monasterii Mulierum, sine clausura viventium, contra praescriptum Decretalis Bonifacii VIII, et Decretorum Concilii Tridentini, nec non Constitutionis S. Pii Papae V, quae incipit: *Circa Pastoralis.*

---

[47] Schaefer, *De Religiosis,* n. 18, p. 15.
[48] Par. 4—*Fontes,* n. 898.

§ 13. Dictarum vero Virginum Conservatoria, licet ab Apostolica Sede, ut praefertur, non approbata, ab hac tamen benigne tolerari. . . . *Quinto, Virgines Anglicanas non esse vere Religiosas; promissiones quae ab ipsis emittuntur, non esse ad summum, nisi Vota simplicia; et transmittendam esse forman, et notificanda verba, quibus dictae promissiones emittuntur. Sexto, Virgines Anglicanas, earumque coetus, esse iurisdictioni ordinariae Episcoporum subditos, in quarum Diocesibus sunt; et ad Ordinarios praedictos pertinere, deputare Directores spirituales, et Confessarios, qui sibi apti videantur, sive ex coetu Presbyterorum Saecularium, sive Regularium.*

XXIII. Cuius rei cum Nos istam in Domino fiduciam habemus, tum illud ad eam perficiendam conducere maxime poterit, si Venerabiles Fratres Ecclesiarum Praesules, in quorum Dioecesibus huiusmodi Instituti Conservatoria, vel iam erecta sunt, vel in posterum erigi contigerit, pias hasce Virgines, in excolenda Dominicae Vineae parte laudabili studio adlaborantes, benigno favore prosequentur, quod Nos eisdem enixe suademus. . .earum vero Conservatorii tolerari quidem ab hac eadem Apostolica Sede, sed Institutum ipsum nec approbatum, nec confirmatum esse; obsistentibus Sacris Canonibus, et generali Constitutione Sancti Pii V, ne Religiosae Mulierum Domus Apostolica confirmatione stabiliantur, quae se perfectae Clausurae legibus non obstrinxerint. . . .

It is noticeable that Benedict XIV does not desire to abrogate the law of Pius V inasmuch as he does not intend to give apostolic approbation to such as lived contrary to that law. Yet he derogates from it to the extent that he acknowledges the passive toleration of these religious congregations, expressly mentioning however, that though the Holy See may approve the rules, it does not wish to approve the institute itself, as in shown by the words, *citra tamen approbationem conservatorii.* These last words are a concession to the law of Pius V, and apparently were added so that a remedy might be at hand in case the evils and abuses feared by Pius should appear; suppression would then be all the easier.[49]

---

[49] Larraona, *Comm. pro Rel.*, I (1920), 47.

There are several points that stand out prominently in this constitution and these will be mentioned briefly. Henceforth these Congregations could approach Rome without the fear of suppression or serious change of their foundation, and even could receive the approval of their rules. Because of their good works the bishops are not to be harsh, but rather benevolent and favorable to them. Above all they were not considered as true religious, that is in the canonical sense, and their vows were recognized as only simple.[50] The document was so clear in setting forth the rights of the Ordinaries in relation to these communities that it became the established guide and norm for all religious congregations until the year 1900.

Rome did not refuse from that time on to approve and confirm the rules of new religious congregations but, until the beginning of the nineteenth century, in approving them she always added the words, *citra tamen approbationem conservatorii*, or some similar phrase.[51] In the beginning the word *Conservatorium* signified a home for poor girls who had been deprived of their parents. There they were carefully provided for, their innocence protected, and their education also assured.[52]

The holy women who took care of these homes naturally would choose one to be the head, at least for the sake of order. Nor is it to be wondered at that in the course of time they should desire to live under some rule, and, since their lives were devoted to so holy a cause, also as religious. But they could not be obliged by the law of the cloister and still do this work of charity and, since solemn vows were permitted only to those who observed the cloister, it can easily be seen that they should profess simple vows without the observance of the cloister. The word *conservatorium* because of this connection later signified those communities of women living together as religious

---

[50] Bouix, *De Jure Reg.*, I, 231.

[51] Larraona, *Comm. pro Rel.*, I (1920), 47, n. 9; Bizzarri, *Collectanea*, p. 743; Benedict XIV, *"Instit. Eccl.,"* 29, n. 13; Vicente, *Instit. Rec.*, n. 98, p. 45.

[52] Bouix, *De Jure Reg.*, I, 329.

under a certain rule yet not obliged to the cloister or to solemn vows. It was synonymous with the term *religious congregation,* which signified a community having the essence of the religious state, but only professing simple vows.[53]

This was an entirely new development in ecclesiastical legislation. As Parsons says:

Down to the time of St. Vincent de Paul (and also S. Angela Merici) it had been generally held that the cloister alone could validly protect those who wished to dedicate their virginity to God; but the new apostle of humanity thought that there were many women who could aid the world while mingling with it, shielded from harm by the love and fear of God.[54]

Coincidentally with the growth of religious congregations another practice grew up whereby the bishops obtained the right to approve of these communities without even consulting Rome. The question may arise about the liceity of this practice in its origin, for once admitting it was illegal a person would likewise be forced to say that actions of this sort were invalid according to the reasons given above with regard to orders. The reason for the doubt arises from the fact that religious congregations were not in existence when the law was made, were not even thought of as such, and, since the legislator knew nothing of them, it might seem that he had no intention of including them in his prohibition. Reasoning thus, one could say the power to approve religious congregations had never been taken away from the bishops. The greater weight of authority is with those who assert that the decrees of the Lateran and Lyons Councils also prohibited the founding of new congregations through the power of the bishop.[55] There

[53] Bouix, *op. cit.,* I 187.

[54] Parsons, *Studies in Church History,* IV, 179.

[55] Bizzarri, *Collectanea,* p. 742; Bouix, *op. cit.,* I, 201: Wernz, *Jus Decret.,* III, n. 608; Concilium prov. Ultrajectensis (1865)—*Coll. Lac.* V., 896-897; Suarez, *De Rel.,* III, L. II, c. 16, n. 8; Smith, *Compendium Juris Canonici,* n. 828; Pejska, *Jus Can. Religiosorum,* p. 13; Piat; *Prael. Jur. Can.* I, q. 23.

are a few nevertheless who deny that this prohibition included congregations.[56]

The reasons for the affirmative are various. The first is from the purpose of the law, *ne nimia religionum diversitas.* Certainly matters would have been worse and the law would have been frustrated and worthless if religious congregations were free to grow after these decrees without papal supervision, as before the decrees. The end the Popes had in view could not have been obtained. Secondly, a decree of John XXII says explicitly that this was not allowed to bishops.[57] It would be exceedingly difficult to maintain that those bodies condemned could have had solemn vows under the authorization only of their bishops, and at the most one could but contend that they were simple, as solemn vows could only be taken in a community approved by the Holy See. These and others were not condemned because they were orders, but because they were illicit attempts at some form of religious life. Thirdly, the word *religio* which was used in the law seems very general, as can be seen from these words, "Religiosus, generale verbum est, et includit omnem professum."[58] From these words it seems apparent that every kind of institute, where profession of the three vows took place, was included in the term *religio.* Finally the constant and almost unanimous consent of authors attribute custom as the source of that power which bishops were considered later on as holding, indicating thereby that previously it was not possessed.

The negative opinion also has arguments in its favor. Vicente sums them up quite well.[59] First, the term *ordo* must be taken in its proper sense, and in this restriction it would

[56] Vicente, *Instit. Rec.,* n. 58, p. 29; Chelodi, *Jus de Personis,* p. 411, footnote n. 1; Toso, *Commentaria Minora,* lb. II, pars II, p. 14.

[57] "Quidem autem eorum dictum habitum et vivendi ritum a quibusdam episcopis seu eorum superioribus vel aliis ecclesiarum praelatis habuisse profitentur, quod nec eis concedere licuit contra forman Concilii Generalis." C. unic. tit. VII, in Extrav. Joan. XXII.

[58] C. 3, *De procuratoribus,* I, 10, in Clem.

[59] *Instit. Rec.,* pp. 27-30.

only include communities with solemn vows. Secondly, a prohibiting and odious law should be restricted and accepted according to the wording of the law, not extended. Thirdly, it is asserted gratis that greater evils would result from the unlimited multiplication of these communities of simple vows than from the unrestricted and uncontrolled growth of orders.

Yet it seems hard to believe that congregations were not included in Innocent's law. It does not suffice to say that a law was odious which was made for the welfare of society without harming or unduly causing suffering to another. Almost all laws would, on this same reasoning, have to be called odious. Rather, it should be said to be favorable since it was for the welfare of the Church and to the harm of no one.[80]

It is true that the words *ordo* and *religio* were used with the older signification, yet that was because there was no other term at hand to describe such communities. Congregations were not religious in the strict sense; and they were not such simply because they lacked papal approbation. To say that they were not religious and hence not forbidden by the Lateran Council and then to say they were not true religious because they had no papal approbation, would be to turn in a vicious circle. All these communities which were vehemently condemned by the Council of Lyons and by John XXII could have rightfully claimed legitimate existence under the plea that they were not true religious, especially as some had received their Ordinary's approval. Any number of communities could have arisen disregarding all commands. Such argument would destroy the law entirely. Besides, as a final argument, it is known that constant opinion and practice denied this power to the several bishops for many centuries.

Conceding that the bishop could not lawfully establish religious congregations after these laws, one must look for the law that gave this right to the bishops, since they did obtain it in the course of time. It is generally admitted that they had

[80] Suarez, *De Rel.*, III, L. II, c. 16, n. 6.

this right about the middle of the eighteenth century. They received it through custom, a constant contrary custom which steadily militated against former legislation. There are in the Church written and unwritten laws, the latter being called custom. Many things are required for the foundation of a law by custom, such as a continuous number of years suffering no interruption, matter that can be prescribed, reasonable actions and the like. What concerns us here mainly is the consent of the proper authority. Any law to have force must come from the proper authority, and custom in order to have the force of law needs the consent of authority.[61]

There are two ways of getting rid of a law by custom, one by connivance, the other by prescription.[62] The method found here is that of prescription. In the case at hand the lawful authority was the Pope. His assent came from the tacit acknowledgment of a practice against the law, which became more and more prevalent, and as time went on more frequent. From the time of Benedict XIV no dissenting voice was heard. After his time authors generally agree that the local Ordinary had this power to establish and approve religious congregations, and this was first received through custom contrary to the general law.[63] It should be stated here that custom derogated only partially from the law, and was against both the law of the Lateran Council and that of Pius. As a consequence the bishop had the power to approve new congregations which was a derogation of Innocent's law; furthermore these communities were not obliged to observe the cloister as had been insisted on in the constitution "*Circa Pastoralis*" of Pius V.

Thus a new law came into being, not written but unwritten, founded only on custom, yet acknowledged by the Supreme

[61] Gommaire Michiels, "De Vi Consuetudinis," *Jus Pontificium*, IV (1924), 178; Vermeersch-Creusen, *Epitome*, I, n. 98.

[62] Ferraris, "Consuetudo", *Bibliotheca Prompta*, II, n. 688.

[63] Piat, *Prael, Jur. Can.*, I, q. 24; Vicente, *Inst. Rea.*, n. 3, p. 4; Bouix, *op. cit.*, I, 326; Wernz, *Jus Decret.*, III, n. 590, footnote n. 15; Larraona *Comm. pro Rel.*, I (1920), 48; Vermeersch, *De Rel.*, I, p. 49; *A. S. S.*, 39, 345, footnote n. 2.

Pontiff, by the practice of the Roman Curia and the almost unanimous consent of canonists. From this time the discretion and power of bringing new congregations to life was left entirely to the bishops. The exact year and date when this practice became lawful and thus had the force of law can not positively be stated. In the beginning it must be admitted the Ordinaries erred and acted both illicitly and invalidly.

Already in 1501 it seems the law was violated, for apparently St. John Valois began his new institute in that year without papal permission but with the consent of the Ordinary.[64] Other examples could be numerated and the number increased in the course of years. Benedict XIV could rightly say in his time that the Tertiaries were in very many places, as there were twelve communities in his city alone and four others in the diocese.[65] These had arisen only with episcopal consent. Before the time of Benedict XIV the practice of the Holy See had been so vacillating and uncertain that during this time it can not be said with certainty that the custom had received the force of law. The words of Benedict XIII in his bull "*Pretiosus*"[66] show the indecision and doubt of the bishops of his time. Besides the continuity of the practice was broken by the succeeding Pope, Clement XII.[67] As a consequence the practice must be said to have received the assurance of a law only after the Constitution "*Quamvis justo*" of Benedict XIV, that is, about the middle of the eighteenth century. His attitude was that he did not approve these institutes but only tolerated them. But by this toleration he also recognized the practice whereby the bishops brought them into existence.

It was but natural that these congregations should turn to their bishops. For lacking the approval of Rome and being unable to obtain it, they were desirous of having some ecclesiastical standing and so received it from their local Ordinary.

[64] Boulx, *De Jure Reg.*, I, 210.
[65] *Inst. Eccles.*, 105, n. 76.
[66] *Bull. Rom.*, XXII, 522, May 25, 1727.
[67] *"Romanus Pontifex,"* Mar. 31, 1732—*Bull. Rom.*, XXIII, 323.

Each Ordinary was interested in the welfare of his own diocese and so ever willing to promote the charitable labors of pious women. Living in common and devoted to a life of charity they also wished to receive the benefits of a religious society. Their labors of mercy would have been cut short, however, had they adhered to the stringent demands of the Constitution of Pius. This, in the main, accounts for the origin of these communities. When one beholds the good work these women were doing and the great benefits which have flowed to the Church from their labors one must admit that the growth of these congregations has been a blessing to the Church. The Holy See soon realized this and seeing that no good would result from their suppression, she gave in for the common good as she always does when such is for the betterment of her children, benignly relaxing the sanctions of her canons.[68]

It is not to be supposed that the new congregations, especially of women, received the favors of the law immediately. They had merely the favor of existence. Among authors there were still many prejudices and many were unwilling to acknowledge their vows.[69] They were not true religious in the sense of the Decretals,[70] and thus all privileges and exemptions of Regulars were denied to them. The bishop's power over them was absolute, and only restrained by justice and restricted by the canons which guarded the rights of the individuals inasmuch as they were persons in the eyes of the law. The attitude of the Holy See was merely passive, permitting their existence, approving their rule of life yet not approving the

---

[68] Pius X. Motu proprio, *"Supremi disciplinae,"* July 12, 1911— *A.A.S.*, III (1911), 005.

[69] Vicente, *Inst. Rec.*, n. 22, p. 10.

[70] Cong. of Bishops and Regulars, *Causa Augustana*, July 2, 1768— Bizzarri, *Collectanea*, 369, n. 5; Vicente, *op. cit.*, n. 7, p. 5; Schaefer, *De Religiosis*, n. 30; Lanslots, *Handbook of Canon Law*, p. 10; Larraona, *Comm. pro Rel.*, I (1920), 175, footnote n. 22. He gives a response of the Congregation of Bishops and Regulars which says the vows of a religious congregation can not be called *vota religiosa* (July 23, 1860), also on p. 176, another response: *"Instituta recentia in quibus vota dumtaxat simplicia emittuntur, hand proprie nomen religionis sibi vindicant."*

institute. These statements are mainly applicable before the nineteenth century.

Much of the prejudice and the objection to these was removed in the nineteenth century. The events of history conspired favorably to the beginnings and the existence of congregations and unfavorably to the existence of orders none of which were founded at this time. Following close upon the heels of the French Revolution conditions in many countries were well nigh unbearable for the old orders which resulted in a change of attitude on the part of the Holy See from passive toleration to definite approbation of religious congregations. The reversal of front is commonly ascribed to the French Revolution.[11] The Napoleonic Code was entirely adverse to solemn vows. Bitter animosity had been stirred up against the ancient orders and this is reflected in laws referring to vows and the capacity to possess worldly goods.[12]

Under ordinary circumstances the law of the State might not have been considered, but in the precarious situation of the Church in France at that time there was grave danger that more serious harm would befall it from lack of observance of the civil law. Conditions were somewhat similar in Belgium where the same law prevailed.[13]

In the United States, which was just a missionary country in the beginning of the nineteenth century, other causes worked favorably for religious congregations. Communities were founded early and the number grew in a short time. Practically all were of women who engaged in school work.[14] Even the nuns of the Order of the Visitation who were bound by the law

[11] Bizzarri, *op. cit.*, 412; Larraona. *Comm. pro Rel.*, I (1920), 50; Fanfani, *De Jure Religiosorum*, p. 7; Piat, *Prael. Jur. Can.*, I, q. 24.

[12] *Lex civilis apud nos* [*France*] *non agnoscit nisi vota simplicia, et quidem ad quinque annos tantum----, qui autem ea emiserunt, servant plenum bonorum dominium: solummodo prohibentur donare sive communitati, sive ejus membris, ultra certam quantitatem a lege determinatam.* Bouix, *op. cit.*, I, 388.

[13] Bouix, *op. cit.*, I, 388.

[14] Sr. Mary Agnes McCann, "Religious Orders of Women of the United States," *Cath. Hist. Rev.*, I (1921), 316-331.

of strict enclosure were permitted by a special indult to engage in teaching.[75] After much discussion as to which communities had simple and which had solemn vows, the Holy See gave an answer September 2, 1864, wherein it was declared that only four monasteries in our country had solemn vows and regarding future ones it decreed in n. V, *In aliis monasteriis, quae in posterum erigentur in omnibus Statibus foederatis, vota Religiosarum nuncupanda sint simplicia.*[76]

This standpoint was adopted generally at this time and all new institutes of the present and the last century take only simple vows, both in this country as well as in all other countries. Because of the changed attitude of the Holy See these institutes were approved without reservation. The words, *citra tamen approbationem conservatorii,* were omitted entirely about the beginning of the last century,[77] signifying the approbation was given fully and without the previous limitations.

Bizzarri gives a list of those approved in the nineteenth century;[78] the earliest approbation by the Congregation of Bishops and Regulars apparently being in 1816. About this time the

[75] *A. S. S.,* I, 709.

[76] A. S. S., I, 739. The attitude of the Church toward solemn vows in our region is of interest here. Difficulties had arisen and perplexing doubts had agitated the minds of confessors relative to the solemnity of the vows of various sisterhoods. Cf. Provincial Council of Cincinnati (1856)—*Coll. Lac.,* III, 209. The Provincial Council of Baltimore (1858) had petitioned Rome to permit institutes with solemn vows in this country (*A. S. S.,* I, 710-711; *Coll. Lac.,* III, 173). Though admitting the civil law did not recognize them, they saw no reason why such professions ought not be made. Objections however were made by non-catholics in America to the cloister as the Archbishop of Baltimore stated in his letter objecting to the obligation of its observance. (Cf. *A. S.* S., I, 712; Bizzarri, *Collectanea,* p. 488, where the objections of the Archbishop of St. Louis because of civil laws are also given.) Prejudice ran high and false reports about enforced stay in these monasteries were spread around so that great clamor was raised by the people. Attempts were made to give access to civil authorities and threats were made to burn the monasteries if a sister were found forced to remain therein. Some of the bishops here differed also as to the expediency of solemn vows because of the need they had for sisters in the education of girls. *Coll. Lac.,* III, 173. It was for these reasons that Rome desired only simple vows for sisters in the United States.

[77] Vecchiotti, *Inst. Can., L.* III, c. 5, § 65; Schaefer, *De Rel.,* n. 13.

[78] Bizzarri, *op. cit.,* 808-814; Vicente, *Instit. Rec.,* pp. 18-27.

practice of approaching Rome for approbation only after a community had been existent for some time came into vogue. For the power of the bishop in approving was so recognized that Rome would not extend its approbation except when the bishop had previously done so, and the institute itself had reached the period of development in which it gave signs of enduring and being beyond the transitory and initial stage of existence. The rapid increase of these communities in our times, especially of sisters, has been phenomenal. This increase is still going on in our days. And what is more surprising the Holy See has been unwilling during the past century to approve any new community with solemn vows; the last order approved was that of the Order of Friars of Penance,[79] confirmed in a brief of Pius VI, *Ex debito pastoralis*, March 27, 1787.[80]

The efforts of Rome in the last century were not towards checking this growth but rather towards directing it and placnig it in the right channels so that the greatest good would result to the Catholic world and to the professed members themselves. More and more she concerned herself with the internal organization of such communities, seeing to it that only such statutes or constitutions were adopted as would further the particular end of the institutes and bring about wholesome government and management of affairs. Much prominence was given to the constitutions, the particular laws of the congregation, so that their approval was looked upon as something greater than the approval of the institute. The complete approbation was only then acquired when these constitutions were stamped with the definite and final approbation of Rome.

At the Vatican Council nothing was done to change the status of affairs. Yet the actions of Pius IX before the Council indicate that he did not view this phenomenal expansion of new congregations over the entire world without some misgivings. In a letter of June 6, 1867, sent to the bishops of the

[79] Larraona, *Comm. pro Rel.*, I (1920), 183; Vermeersch, *De Rel.*, I, n. 57; Schaefer, *De Rel.*, n. 64.

[80] *Bull. Rom. Continuatio,* II, 1782.

world to find out the opinions of various sections of the globe and to determine definitely the *agenda* of the Council, he proposed the following question in n. 10:

Plures prodierunt et in dies prodeunt Congregationes et Instituta virorum et mulierum, qui votis simplicibus obstricti, piis muneribus obeundis se addicunt. Expeditne ut potius Congregationes ab Apostolica Sede probatae augeantur latius et crescant, quam ut novae eumdem prope finem habentes constituantur et efformentur?[81]

Thus he apparently had some doubts about the value of this increase and was desirous of knowing whether the bishops thought that the institutes already founded should rather grow and increase in number, or whether new ones should be established though they had well nigh the same purpose in view. The question seems to have died right here, as the sudden unexpected dissolution of the Council did not permit discussion on this point to take place. France is the only country on record which responded directly to the question.[82] Her postulates were given by several bishops in 1869. The answer leaves no doubt as to their position. Their response was given in these words:

Longissime abest, ut religosarum mulierum numerus, quae iuventutis educationi, infirmorum visitationi, et curae aliisque operibus misericordiae, tum in urbibus, tum in ruralibus paroeciis, vacant, sufficiens sit. Quantumvis igitur hujus generis instituta, hoc praesertim saeculo, multiplicata sint, novis fundationibus, nedum obsistendum, favendum e contra, positis ponendis, videtur.[83]

This answer was clear, the number should be increased, not diminished. Of all the countries of the Catholic world France seems to be the only one that found it frequently necessary to repeat the law that episcopal consent was necessary before a religious congregation could be founded. At least this might

[81] *Coll. Lac.*, VII, 1028.

[82] The bishops of Belgium and Holland answered indirectly by praising the new congregations and extolling their great utility. *Coll. Lac.*, VII, 877 a.

[83] *Coll. Lac.*, VII, 837 a.

be inferred from so many repetitions of the law by various particular councils.[84] These frequent repetitions may have had their origin in the desire to clarify and express a general law which was not written in the canons of the Church, as it grew out of custom, but it seems they may have been evoked because of many violations. The Plenary Council of Latin America (1899) also found cause to repeat this law.[85]

As regards the Orientals there is little to be said. At the time of the promulgation of the decrees of the Council of the Lateran they were separated from the Church. Various branches and nationalities came back later to the Church, but she was careful not to impose the majority of her disciplinary measures on them. Thus it can be said that the Council of the Lateran did not oblige those who returned. Such also was the actual practice. For the authority of these Uniates is still grounded in the Council of Chalcedon, as can be seen from the canons of the Synod of Mt. Lebanon (1736) which decreed: "Non possunt nova erigi monasteria sine consensu Ordinarii loci, ut sacra praecipit Calcedonensis Synodus."[86]

The conditions among the Orientals were not the same as in the Latin rite, since in the latter the growth of new congregations, being spontaneous, needed no urging; whereas for the former the Popes found it expedient to urge a steadier and more fervent growth. It was because of this that Pius IX, April 8, 1862, addressed an Encyclical letter to the patriarchs and bishops of the Orient asking them to determine upon means to increase the number of religious families in their territories.[87]

[84] Concil. Prov. Burdigalensis, (1850), *Coll. Lac.*, IV, 603; Concil. Prov. Turonensis (1849), *Coll. Lac.*, IV, 278 d; Concil. Prov. Remensis (1849), *Coll. Lac.*, IV, 144; Concil. Prov. Rothomagensis (1850), *Coll. Lac.*, IV, 532 d; Concil. Prov. Ultrajectensis (1865), *Coll. Lac.*, V, 896-897; Concil. Prov. Pragensis (1860), *Coll. Lac.*, V, 572 b.

[85] *Acta et Decreta Concilii Plen. Latinae Americae*, n. 822.

[86] *Coll. Lac.*, II, 355.

[87] *Coll. Lac.*, II, 560 b.

Article II

The Fourth Period.

The fourth period of our history finds no change in the substance of the law that prevailed at the end of the third period, for to this day the power of approving religious congregations is retained by the bishops. The inauguration of a new era consisted in the clarifying of issues and doubts and in a certain limitation of this episcopal power by the exacting of special conditions before the foundation of a new religious institute.

It is Leo XIII who gave rise to this period through his Constitution, "*Conditae a Christo*," of December 8, 1900,[88] which constitution is considered as having given the juridical character to these religious congregations,[89] and also as being their Magna Charta.[90] The purpose of the constitution was to determine specifically the respective rights of religious congregations in their relations to the local Ordinary, especially of those communities which had received papal approbation. There are two parts to the constitution, the first treating of the power of the bishop in the establishment of religious congregations, whilst the second part regulates the interior organization of those communities already praised or approved by Rome. The first part is of concern here. It is the first direct legal written recognition by a Pope of the power of the bishops to approve religious congregations.

Paragraph 1, n. I. Episcopi est quamlibet recens natam sodalitatem non prius in dioecesim recipere, quam leges ejus constitutionesque cognorit itemque probarit; si videlicet neque fidei honestative morum, neque sacris canonibus et Pontificum decretis adversentur, si apte statuto fini conveniant.

---

[88] *Fontes*, n. 644.
[89] Larraona, *Comm. pro Rel.*, I (1920), 171, n. 17.
[90] Vicente, *Instit. Rec.*, n. 4, p. 4.

II. Domus nulla novarum sodalitatum iusto jure fundabitur, nisi annuente probante Episcopo. Episcopus vero fundandi veniam ne impertiat, nisi inquisitione diligenter acta quales sint qui id poscant: an recte probeque sentiant, an prudentia praediti, an studio divinae gloriae, suaeque et alienae salutis praecipue ducti.

III. Episcopi, quoad fieri possit, potius quam novam in aliquo genere sodalitatem condant vel approbent, utilius unam quamdam adsciscent de iam approbatis, quae actionis institutum profiteatur adsimile.

These comprise the principal points of interest to us. The rest of the constitution is taken up with various other qualities that should be had, namely a special end, the necessary means of sustenance and the like. The second part consists in the defining of the specific rights of both the Bishops and the congregations. This letter is the beginning of the tendency to check the power of the bishop to some extent. His power in substance is the same as before. But now he must observe certain conditions before he can rightfully give existence to a new community. Some forms of religious life which were not in accordance with Rome's ideal were arising, and apparently there had been a too indiscriminate growth. The bishops were admonished to act more cautiously, not to erect a new one unless it was deemed necessary and only when no similar institute already approved could be obtained.

Shortly after, as a supplement to this constitution, the Congregation of Bishops and Regulars issued a pamphlet on June 28, 1901, which is generally referred to as the *Normae*.[91] In this the Sacred Congregation outlines a program of formation and a process for obtaining the approbation of the Church.[92] It is based upon the experience of the previous hundred years, with a view of instructing bishops as to the nature of the vows, form of government of religious congregations and

[91] The full title is: *Normae Secundum Quas S. Cong. Episcoporum et Regularium Procedere Solet in Approbandis Novis Institutis Votorum Simplicium.*

[92] *American Eccles. Review,* 26 (1902), 594.

other things of general concern. In no sense did it have the force of law,[93] as its title indicates in using the word *solet*. But the observance of these regulations would expedite matters considerably when these congregations sought Rome's approbation. They are of practical value nowadays even though they have been supplanted partly by the new Code and partly by the new *Normae* of the Congregation of Religious, published in 1921.[94] Yet as these later *Normae* refer explicity to the earlier *Normae*, those of 1901 still serve as a guide.

Only a few years later this power of the Ordinaries was again partially modified by Pius X in his Motu Proprio, "*Dei providentis*," of July 16, 1906.[95] He found it expedient to oblige the bishops to consult the Holy See before permitting a new religious congregation to be established. He gives as a reason the fear that too many of these institutes might bring injury to ecclesiastical discipline and thus cause confusion. He says furthermore that the Constitution of Leo XIII[96] and the *Normae* (1901) have not amply provided for the proper establishment of these institutes. More rules were needed to check the growth, and since in some cases the judgment of the bishops was faulty, hereafter the final judgment as to the necessity and opportuneness of a new religious congregation was to rest with the Holy See.[97] So to remedy the evils he saw and the defects in the regulations of Leo XIII, he decreed:

I. Nullus Episcopus aut cujusvis loci Ordinarius, nisi habita Apostolicae Sedis per litteras licentia, novam alterutrius sexus sodalitatem condat aut in sua dioecesi condi permittat.

II. Ordinarius, hujus licentiae impetrandae gratia, Sacrorum Consilium Episcoporum et Regularium negotiis praeposi-

[93] Piat, *Prael. Jur. Can.*, I, q. 2; Vicente, *op. cit.*, n. 91, p. 42; Vermeersch, *De Rel.*, II, 130, n. 6.

[94] Normae (1921), *A. A. S.*, XIII (1921), 312-319. Cf. Vermeersch, "De Conscribendis Constit." *Periodica*, XVI (1927), 41, 107, 154.

[95] *Fontes*, n. 675.

[96] "*Conditae a Christo*," Dec. 8, 1900—Fontes, n. 644.

[97] Larraona, *Comm. pro Rel.*, I (1920), 134, footnote n. 13.

tum adeat per libellum supplicem, quo haec docebit: quis qualisque sit novae sodalitatis auctor, et qua in causa ad eam instituenduam ducatur; quibus verbis conceptum sit sodalitatis condendae nomen seu titulus; quae sit forma, color, materia, partes habitus a novitiis et professis gestandi; quot et quaenam sibi opera sodalitas assumptura sit; quibus opibus tuitio eiusdem contineatur; an similia in diocesi sint instituta, et quibus illa operibus insistant.

III. Accepta Sacri Consilii venia, nihil iam obstabit, quominus Ordinarius novam sodalitatem instituat aut institui permittat, eo tamen titulo, habitu, proposito ceterisque rebus ab ipso Sacro Consilio recognitis, probatis designatisve: quae numquam deinceps, nisi eodem consentiente, immutari licebit.

IV. Conditae sodalitatis constitutiones Ordinarius recognoscat: verum ne prius approbet, quam eas ad normam eorum, quae Sacrum Consilum in hac causa decrevit, exigendas curaverit.

Pius X did not then take this power away from the bishops but demanded that they consult the Holy See before they found or permit a new institute to be founded. But besides this many restrictions were placed upon the use of this power. In approaching the Congregation of Bishops and Regulars they had to give the name of the institute and the founder, the reasons for its foundation, its scope, and the form of the habit. They also were to tell whether similar institutes were already in the diocese. Evidently this was to place a check on the creation of new religious congregations without sufficient cause. Furthermore what the Holy See had recognized in any way could no longer be changed solely at the discretion of the Ordinary. And lastly, before he gives these congregations his approbation he is obliged to see to it that the new constitutions are in harmony with the norms laid down by the Congregation of Bishops and Regulars. The new Code departed but little from this law as the Code was compiled mainly in accordance with the wishes of Pius X. Since the laws are so similar, a more thorough explanation will be given in the commentary, in chapter four.

During all this time no new statutes were put in force relative to the foundation of new orders. The law of the IV Lateran Council was never abrogated by law or custom and, in later years, it was admitted by all authorities that the only competent power to establish an order was the Holy See; and this is also admitted after the new Code. To sum up in a few words, before the new Code the proper authority to establish an order was the Supreme Pontiff, whereas for a congregation the will of the bishop sufficed to give it legal existence. These same principles are also a part of the law today.

CHAPTER III

Article 1

THE NATURE OF APPROBATION

Before beginning a commentary on the present law it will be useful to know the meaning and purpose of the word *approbation*, both in its general signification and also in its particular connotations, the latter being especially of much interest to us. The word *approbation* is formed from a combination of the Latin forms *ad* and *probare* and is defined as an assent given after weighing and balancing something in one's judgment.[1] If, however, such an assent is given to any public act by one in authority and in an official capacity, approbation then imports an official sanction, ratification and favorable judgment. It would therefore indicate that, having viewed a certain actuality or proposal, the authority is assured it is in harmony with the polity and purpose of that office entrusted to his care as guardian of the public good. Thus he approves publicly of that which is sought.

However, the concern here is not so much with the general meaning of the word as with its ecclesiastical meaning and the particular signification which it has to the topic now under discussion. *Approbation* as defined in the New Catholic Dictionary is; *an act by which a legitimate superior authorizes an ecclesiastic actually to exercise his ministry.*[2] Such definition certainly does not apply here as these words, when used by the Church, embody the general signification of the word as

[1] Forcellini, *Totius Latinitatis Lexicon*, I, 341.
[2] *The New Catholic Dictionary*, p. 59.

generally used. Transferring the prevailing thought of the definition and applying it to religious institutes one may say that approbation is an act by which a legitimate superior judges a new institute to be both conducive to the perfection of its members and to the welfare of the Church; and through this judgment he establishes the community as such giving it its special laws. As for the first approbation the consequence of this judgment and this is the most important effect, will be the actual creation of the institute into a moral ecclesiastical person through the efficacious will of the lawful superior.[4] As a consequence those attributes necessary for the religious state, together with all the privileges of religious, are conferred on the religious community.

Three things are thus included in the approbation of an institute: first, canonical existence is granted to the religious institute; secondly, there is an authentic judgment that such a religious life is good, lawful and useful;[5] thirdly, power is given to the superiors of that community to receive the vows of religion from the members and thus establish them as true religious. This holds good for the approbation granted by the Holy See or the Bishop, for while there exist differences between papal approbation and episcopal approbation, nevertheless the notes mentioned here are common to both. It can be truly said that this approbation is the result of mature deliberation after which an authentic declaration is made that such a life is free from heresy or superstition, its purpose in view is laudable, the general means proposed are in themselves capable of leading to sanctification.

It is but natural that the pronouncement of the Church relative to new institutes should have as a purpose the declaration that the life as mapped out for the new institute leads to sanctification. The primary purpose of all religious life is individual perfection, the approximation of the soul to God

---

[4] Suarez, *De Rel.*, III, L. II, c. 15, n. 11.

[5] Fanfani, *De Jure Relig.*, n. 9; Piat, *Prael. Juris Reg.*, q. 22; Wernz, *Jus Decr.*, III, n. 590.

through charity,[6] in which however the Church has no unimportant part. And as the people in the world need ecclesiastical guidance on the road to perfection, so the religious life, which seeks a higher plane, demands more special guidance and direction. The principal stress of ecclestiastical appromation tends to the declaration that the life is directly conducive to sanctity. To some extent the approval may be compared to the ecclesiastical canonization of saints. As canonization does not confer sanctity upon the saint neither does the Church's approbation give holiness to the religious institute. In either case nothing is added to the perfection or sanctity, but there is added the external proclamation of the holiness of the individual or of the institute's scope.[7] As a consequence it could happen in time that the members of the institute as a body would not tend to perfection, but that would arise from actions contrary to the spirit and guiding principle of the institute, that is through abuses and depraved morals.[8] The approbation of the Church then has nothing to do with the declaration of sanctity of the members since holiness is contingent upon the special efforts of the individuals.

It is necessary, however, to understand that the Church does not hold herself merely negatively, as she does in the approval by the *imprimatur* of books. For in the approval of books she usually declares that nothing is contained therein that needs reproof, or *nihil obstat* as is generally found.[9] The judgment is a positive assertion that the intention of the institute is upright, that the institute will lead to sanctification, and with this judgment permission is also given for all things necessary that the community might enjoy existence.

The necessity of the Church's approval is patent from positive law, yet irrespective of positive law one may ask whether approval is demanded by the divine law. Would it be necessary to have ecclesiastical approbation in order to be a

[6] St. Thomas, 2, 2, Q. 186, art. 3.
[7] Piat, *op. cit.*, Q. 18, p. 7; Suarez, *op. cit.*, III, L. II, c. 15, n. 2.
[8] Suarez, *op. cit.*, III, L. II, c. 17, n. 21.
[9] Vicente, *Rec. Inst.*, n. 28.

true religious community if the law of the Church did not exist? Authors disagree as to its necessity through divine law. The prevailing opinion affirms divine law requires a new institute have some approbation in order to make it truly religious.[10] The question is merely theoretical and has no practical value as the positive law of today covers all cases.

Two things are found in each religious institute, the essence of religion itself which consists in the three vows, and the determination of this essence to a certain manner of life. The essence of the religious state has its foundation in the Gospels and under this aspect does not require any ecclesiastical approbation.[11] It is from the other viewpoint, the adaptation of the Gospels to a particular form of life, that authors generally admit that considering the intrinsic nature of an institute some approval of the Church is required. The arguments for both sides are aptly summed up by Piat, Suarez, and Bouix, in the citations noted above. Examining their meaning, one draws the conclusion that institutes do not intrinsically require positive, but tacit approbation, that is, that approbation through which the Church acknowledges their existence and shows by her actions that she holds them in high esteem. If positive approbation were demanded it would be hard to understand the status of the early monastic institutes of which some surely never received any explicit approval from legitimate authority.

From the nature of things it can be rightfully said that this approbation does not necessarily belong to the Pope. *Per se* it belongs also to the bishop.[12] He is the proper authority in his diocese and has the care of souls. Besides no reason can be brought why pontifical approbation is required. Pontifical approbation is required in certain cases but only because positive law demands it. That this power belongs *per se* to the bishop can be seen from the constant practice of the Church

[10] Piat, *Prael. Jur. Reg.*, Q. 18, p. 7; Fanfani, *De Jure Reg.*, p. 6; Schaefer, *De Rel.*, p. 34, footnote; Suarez, *op. cit.*, III, L. II, c. 15, n. 10.

[11] Bellarminus, L. II, *De Mon.*, C. 4.

[12] Suarez, *op. cit.*, III, L. II, c. 17, n. 5; Conc. Colocensis, (1863)—*Coll. Lac.*, V, 688 d; Schmalzgrueber, *Jus Eccles. Universum*, n. 22, q. 5.

which for centuries permitted it to be exercised by bishops, putting an end to it only when evils became so great that a higher authority was deemed necessary. One should have no difficulty to understand that at times it may be necessary for the Holy See to step in and to withdraw certain powers from inferiors, especially when affairs are such as to threaten imminent danger to the Church or individuals, as in reality it did withdraw this power from the local Ordinaries in the thirteenth century.

Granted this concurrence of power in both the bishop and the Pope one must not suppose that their power is the same, or that the effects are identical as far as their approbations are concerned. All power of ruling is greater in the Supreme Pontiff than in the bishop. So in this power of approbation authors point out many differences. The differences consist principally in the following: first, this power of approving is possessed by the Supreme Pontiff in a higher manner than by the bishops since to him alone belongs the plenitude of power;[13] secondly, the approbation of the bishop is fallible, whereas that of the Pope when given personally and definitely is truly infallible;[14] thirdly, the approbation of the Pope is not subject to the judgment of another and is consequently not apt to be changed by another; but the approbation of the bishop is subject to the scrutiny of the Pope, and being subject to the judgment of the Pope it can be restricted or totally suspended;[15] finally, the Pope can approve *simpliciter*, the bishop *secundum quid*, since the latter's power has many limitations and is in accordance with the will of his superior. The bishop's power likewise is restricted to his diocese and can not extend to territory beyond his diocese as that is outside of his jurisdiction. Besides it lacks the firmness and stability that comes

[13] Suarez, *op. cit.*, III, L. II, c. 17, n. 15.
[14] Suarez, *op. cit., loc. cit.;* Bouix, *De Reg.*, I, 195, 239.
[15] Suarez, *De Rel.*, III, L. II, c. 17, n. 15; Bouix, *De Reg.*, I, 195. This is shown by the fact that the Pope can approve an institute with solemn vows, whereas that power is not now conceded to the bishops.

only from Papal approbation.[16] This is amply demonstrated in the practice that prevails today. The episcopal approval is considered temporary not final, and only as a step to a higher approval; sufficient for a time but because of its limitations and many deficiencies religious communities consider it more expedient later to obtain Papal approbation, since so many benefits accrue therefrom.

A word must be said here about the infallibility of the Pope in approving religious institutes. The question may be rightly asked whether the Pope can err in giving his solemn commendation to a religious society. Here, above all else one must consider solely Papal approval since the gift of infallibility is conferred only on the Pope, and being a personal prerogative it can not be delegated to another. The individual bishops themselves are fallible and one may safely admit the possibility of error in their judgment, so that it is possible for them to approve that which is heretical. Theologians are in agreement that the Pope's definite approbation has the stamp of infallibility.[17] The reasons given for this infallibility are, as it were, corollaries to the general dogma of the Church. Because the Church is indefectible she could not be in error in approving a religious institute since the welfare of so many would be thereby affected.[18] If the Pope were able to err in such matters it would be detrimental to the entire Church.

It remains to explain the meaning and to determine the extent of this infallibility. The approbation must be given without any restrictions, definitely and not temporarily, in a solemn form and by the Pope himself. Certainly the three vows which are common to all religious communities need not fall under this judgment, as they already have the com-

[16] Suarez, *op. cit.*, III, L. II, c. 17, n. 30; Laurentius, *Inst. Jur. Ecc.*, n. 779; Concilium Prov. Avenionensis (1849)—*Coll. Lac.*, IV, 351 c.

[17] Pesch, *Praelectiones Dogmaticae*, I, 544; Hurter, *Theologia Dogmatica*, n. 278; Mazzella, *De Religione et Ecclesia*, n. 814; Tanquerey, *Synopsis Theologiae Dogmaticae*, I, n. 841.

[18] Pesch, *op. cit.*, I, 546.

mendation of Christ.[19] Besides the counsels which are common to all, each community has its own particular scope and rules, and the judgment of the Pope centers around the uprightness and probity of the scope and rules, declaring that nothing harmful is contained to faith or morals and also asserting that they will lead to santification if faithfully followed.[20] It is in this that the Pope is infallible. The only safe conclusion that one may hold is that an institute and rule that have received the Pope's solemn approval must be considered as an absolutely safe guide to perfection.

There is another judgment contained in approbation and that judgment relates to prudence in the guidance of ecclesiastical affairs. Is it always good and for the welfare of society that a religious institute be established at any time and place? Likewise one may ask whether it is not sometimes inexpedient, and whether the Church by proclaiming such an institute opportune and useful enjoys infallibility? Authors are divided on this point and as a consequence it is difficult to say that the establishment of a new religious institute is always opportune.[21] Nevertheless, it is plain that one may be close to heresy if he should state the negative and were to say that at any time the foundation of a certain institute was in any way inexpedient or harmful. Thus Pius VI condemned the errors of the Synod of Pistoia which are closely related to the point under discussion.[22] In another instance Wickliffe was also condemned by the

[19] Pesch, *op. cit.*, I, 544.

[20] Bouix, *De Reg.*, I, 237; Suarez, *De Rel.*, III, L. II, c. 15, n. 13.

[21] Mazzella, *De Religione et Ecclesia*, n. 814.

[22] For the proscribed proposition n. 82 of the Synod of Pistoia reads: "Multiplicationem ordinum ac diversitatem naturaliter inferre perturbationem et confusionem, item in eo quod praemittet regularium fundatores, qui post monastica instituta prodierunt, ordines superaddentes ordinibus, reformationes reformationibus nihil aliud fecisse, quam primariam mali causam magis magisque dilatare"; Pius VI says: "intellecta de ordinibus et institutis a Sancta Sede probatis, quasi distincta piorum munerum varietas, quibus distincti ordines addicti sunt, natura sua, perturbationem et confusionem pareri debeat:—falsa, calumniosa, in sanctos fundatores eorumque fideles alumnos, tum et in ipsos summos Pontifices iniuriosa."—Denzinger, *Enchiridion*, n. 1582.

Council of Constance because he dared to condemn the approved religious institutes.[23]

Theologians refer only to religious orders when speaking about this prerogative of infallibility in the Pope, but no reason exists why the same should not be said of religious congregations. Formerly only orders received the definite papal approbation in solemn form but since the new Code this honor will not be denied to religious congregations. Furthermore, it must be remembered that Roman Congregations which give this approval in the name of the Holy Father are not included in this claim of infallibility even when with the consent of the Pope himself they issue a decree of approbation. It is only when the Pope approves these institutes personally, finally and definitely, e. g., by a constitution or a *Motu Proprio,* or a decree issued in solemn form, that we can speak of infallibility.

Article 2

The Variety of Religious Institutes

The greater contact one makes with the Catholic Church and the various religious communities the more one is amazed at the great variety of institutions approved by the Church. With this great variety prevalent many find it hard to understand why new institutes should be constantly granted recognition by the Church. Besides, the growth of new communities, where there is need for them, is always being encouraged by the Holy See. To understand this attitude of the Church it is necessary to comprehend fully how one institute differs from another. Oftentimes it is very difficult to know wherein this variety really consists, to explain this diversity and to realize its practical value. They all are designated under the term

[23] Suarez, *op. cit.,* III, L. II, c. 17, n. 18.

religious and so must have something in common, yet withal there are so many diversifications in evidence.[24]

A full understanding of this diversity will arise only when one grasps the purpose or end of religious life. The aim and scope of religious life is Christian perfection.[25] And, though essentially, this aim is discernible in the observance of the commandments, yet it is instrumentally, to be found especially in the counsels. Through the three vows the professed promises to strive for perfection which consists in union with God. As one who enters a school professes a desire for knowledge, so one who enters the religious fold expresses his eagerness to obtain perfection.[26] The three vows are considered as the most useful means to this perfection since they remove the chief impediments to sanctity.[27] All religious agree in this aim at personal sanctification. They differ chiefly in their scope or their secondary end and in the means employed to observe the three vows and to obtain their special end.[28] Two reasons then are generally given for the distinction of one religious institute from another. The diversity arises from two sources: first, from the proper and peculiar end of the institute which generally expresses the reason for which that certain institute was

[24] The present Pontiff, Pius XI, expressed most beautifully the import of this variety in these words: "Etenim, quamquam una atque individua est religiosae vitae natura, multiplices tamen ea formas induit, cum ex Sodalitatibus aliae aliter deo serviant, aliae alia caritatis beneficentiaeque opera, ad maiorem Dei gloriam proximorumque utilitatem, instituto suo persequantur. Ex hac igitur tanta religiosorum Ordinum varietate, quasi ex dissimilibus arboribus in agro dominico consitis, magna oritur et in salutem gentium provenit fructuum varietas; atque nihil sane pulchrius atque adspectu delectabilius quam harum complexus atque universitas Sodalitatum, quae, etsi ad unum atque idem denique spectant, habent tamen suum quaeque industriae et laboris campum, a ceteris aliqua ex parte distinctum. Fieri enim divinae Providentiae consilio solet, ut, quotiescumque novis est necessitatibus occurrendum, nova item religiosa instituta excitentur ac floreant."—Apostolic Letter, "*Unigenitus Dei,*" March 19, 1924—*A. A. S.*, XVI (1924), 133.

[25] Schaefer, *De Rel.*, n. 53; Wernz, *Jus Dec.*, III, n. 592.

[26] St. Thomas, 2, 2, q. 186, art. 2.

[27] Bellarminus, L. II, *De Monach.*, c. 2.

[28] Ferraris, *Bibliotheca*, VI, p. 090, n. 17.

established; and, secondly, from the different means and spiritual exercises by which it tends to this end, and the means it uses in the observance of the vows."[29]

A distinction does exist but it is not a distinction of kind, but one might say of species. The primary and general end, which is common to all, is the sanctification of the members by the observance of the three vows and the constitutions; whereas the secondary end proper to each institute consists in peculiar works of charity for which the institute itself has been especially formed.[30]

Oftentimes historical reasons give cause for distinction. If the religious orders of the first eight centuries are considered, it is found that the communities differed mainly in their origin and the rule observed. Later orders arose with the avowed purpose of reforming the deteriorated older orders.[31] In time military orders arose with the expressed purpose of defending and recovering the Holy Land. Later communities were founded especially to cultivate the ideal of poverty, to redeem captives, to teach, to aid the needy in suffering, and to work in foreign lands. And finally there is the great multiplication of congregations which has been so marked in the past two centuries, which embrace almost every imaginable work of charity on this earth. The roots of all these are found in the times of their beginning. A need was felt in the Church, a deficiency was somehow noticeable, and soon willing souls were found to provide for the need, and to labor and strive not only for their own perfection but also for the welfare of others.

The discovery of new lands and countries also had its influence on the growth of new institutes, and also the revival of the faith in places where it had been partially destroyed through persecution, such especially being the case in France

[29] Schmalzgrueber, *Jus Eccles.*, Lib. 4, tit. 31, n. 7; St. Thomas, 2, 2, q. 188, art. 1; Fagnanus, L. III, P. II, *De Reg.*, cap. *Sane*, n. 12, 13, 14.

[30] *Normae.* (1901), n. 42. 43.

[31] Vecchiotti, *Inst. Can.*, L. III, c. 9, 87, p. 362.

in the middle of the past century. In a newly founded country the bishops always realized the necessity of religious congregations and it was this need which accounts for the origin of most of the communities in the United States.[32] Distance and inability to communicate readily with the mother house in foreign lands also had its influence and several of our present independent communities were formerly part of some older communities in Europe.[33] In many instances our bishops favored the establishment of religious communities whose members were native to the country and could adapt their rule of life to present conditions. In this respect preference was shown to the newer congregations better equipped to minister to the local needs in the field of education and charity.[34] Or it happened that a certain nationality was being spiritually neglected and the bishop seeing this established a community especially suited to serve the needs of that nationality.[35] It can be safely said that the same causes which operated here were in evidence in other countries and under similar circumstances.

This variety also has its foundation in the nature of man himself. It could hardly be possible that the same manner of life could be suitable to everyone, as men differ in their inclinations and propensities.[36] And it is to the lasting glory of the Church that she can say to anyone desirous of embracing the religious life that there is open to him a field best suited to his inclinations irrespective of what he may desire to accomplish. There is hardly a field of Christian charity imaginable which is not already being provided for by some existing religious institute. It is thus the beauty and order of the Church shows at its best, for in all this diversity one

[32] Sr. Mary Agnes McCann, "Religious Orders of Women of the United States," *Cath. Hist. Rev.*, I (1921), 310-331.

[33] Sr. Mary Agnes McCann, *op. cit.*,—I (1921), 324.

[34] "The Recent Regulations Regarding the Canonical Institution of New Religious Communities," *Amer. Eccles. Rev.*, XXVI (1902), 590-594.

[35] "Polish Religious Communities," *Amer. Ecc. Rev.*, XXVI, (1902), 215.

[36] Aquilar, *Scientiae Juridicae*, p. 268; Bellarminus, L. II, *De Monach.*, c. 3; Piat, *Prael Jur. Reg.*, I, q. 30.

spirit is discerned.[37] God, in a providential manner, has provided for every phase of human desire and longing for perfection.

Yet, though the Church has not ceased to praise this growth and variety of religious communities and to extol their work,[38] she does not accept new institutes in her fold without sufficient reason, nor is she over-desirous of seeing a too great diversification. It is true at present to say that proposed new communities are not looked upon with favor in the eyes of the law.[39] Their need and necessity must be shown and then only are they welcomed by the Church. The mind of the Church is, that it is better for few religious communities to exist rich in numbers, piety and charity, than that many exist weak and hardly able to stand; and it is better that those existing be encouraged and increased than that new ones be instituted.[40] Therefore too great a variety will be checked rather than promoted by the Church. The reason is expressed also by Pius X who says that the intemperate growth of these communities would bring great disturbance into the Church.[41]

The necessity of the new institute must be shown, its adaptability to its surroundings must be considered and, if institutions similar in scope are to be found nearby and are available for the work, these should be used and not a new one created.[42] On the other hand, if the need is fully shown, the Church will give her permission and allow a new institute

[37] Aquilar, *Scientiae Juridicae*, p. 268.

[38] Vecchiotti, *Inst. Can.*, L. III, c. 9, m. 87, p. 362.

[39] Pejska, *Jus Can. Rel.*, p. 12.

[40] Concil. Prov. Burdigalensis, 1850—*Coll. Lac.*, IV, 603 b; Concil. Prov. Bituricensis, 1850—*Coll. Lac.*, IV, 1100 b; Concil. Prov. Remensis, 1849—*Coll. Lac.*, IV, 144 b; Concil. Prov. Albiensis, 1850—*Coll. Lac.*, IV, 410 b; Concil. Prov. Senonensis, 1850—*Coll. Lac.*, IV, 908 a. Confer also the Constitution of Leo XIII, *Conditae a Christo*, n. 3: "Episcopi quoad fieri possit, potius quam novam in aliquo genere sodalitatem condant vel approbent, utilius unam quandam adscissent de iam approbatis, quae actionis institutum profiteatur ac simile."—*Fontes*, n. 644.

[41] Constitution, *Dei providentis*, July 16, 1906—*Fontes*, n. 675.

[42] Vicente, *Inst. Rec.*, n. 69.

to be established. This standpoint should not be misinterpreted, since it is based upon the experience of years and has the welfare of the entire Church at heart, nor does it in any way hinder a person from embracing the religious life.

Of course much depends on the number of communities already established in a certain region. If there is an abundance and the existing communities provide amply for all the needs of the locality, the Holy See would be unwilling to see a new community founded, preferring to see the older ones more solidly established. But if religious communities should be few in number consent will be more readily given as then the need is more evident. In the past many communities have arisen which differed from one another solely in their origin and regime. The same secondary end or scope is discernible, and the only difference noticeable is a difference in rule and this distinction in fact is very slight.[43] The Church does not desire this too close identity of religious communities henceforth, but good reasons may permit it even in the future. The extent of most institutes is very limited in territory and so it need not surprise us that there arise in different countries communities whose sole distinction might be said to be in the fact that they are actually distinct corporate bodies, that is, independent but similar societies agreeing in the secondary end and having somewhat similar rules. The real issue in the mind of the Church is the local necessity and, if a new religious community can ameliorate the unsatisfactory conditions, the Holy See is willing to encourage the institute for the welfare of that section.

At present a middle pathway has been chosen between the absolute prohibition of new communities, as suggested before the Vatican Council,[44] and the conditions of the nineteenth century when this growth was subject to no check at all. The latter condition gave results which the Holy See viewed with

[43] Wernz, *Jus Decret.*, III, n. 592.

[44] Letter of Pius IX to the bishops of the world before the convening of the Vatican Council—*Coll. Lac.*, VII, 1028; VII, 837 a. Vide supra, p. 67.

alarm. In order that the bishop might act more cautiously, many suggestions and limitations were made and a law promulgated demanding consultation with the Holy See before any new foundation. The spirit that animates the Church in this matter should also animate the local Ordinary. Before giving his consent the local Ordinary should also consider the mind of the Holy See and endeavor to see that the norms laid down as a guidance be in all their details his guide.

History teaches us that the founders of religious institutes have acted not of their own initiative but have been prompted by the Holy Spirit to do some special good in the world through a new order or congregation.[45] *Per se* any one of the faithful, man or woman, may place his request before an ecclesiastical authority to obtain the right to establish a new congregation provided he is divinely called.[46] For surely, if a special vocation is necessary, as some claim, for the religious life,[47] *a fortiori* it should be demanded of him who establishes and lays the foundation of such life. At least this would seem to be more consonant with sound principles, since his institution is to be the guide for many souls, and since the call to be a founder ought to be more special than the general invitation to follow Christ. Certainly no wordly desire, ambition or pride should be the motivating causes. The love of God as evidenced in the saintly founders of the past ages, should be the only compelling influence to move him to found an institute whose sole object should be to further the sanctification of men.

It is not to be thought that the founder is free to act independently of ecclesiastical authority. The welfare of society demands the proper regulation of all things and for this reason the bishop of the diocese, who is the only proper authority here must be approached and all things should be made known to him and his permission thus obtained. The

---

[45] Wernz, *Jus Dec.*, III, n. 599.
[46] Fanfani, *De Jure Rel.*, p. 6.
[47] Piat, *Prael. Jur. Reg.*, q. 39.

bishop will then seek the motives, the reasons that lead to do this, the nature of the undertaking and its necessity and utility.[48] Neither should permission be granted without due deliberation but rather an investigation of the person's character, habits and ability should be immediately started so that the bishop may learn all that is desired and required by the Holy See. Above all everything should be done under the authority of the bishop and he alone will be the true judge of the necessity, utility, and practicality of the proposed institute. If for any reason his reply should be in the negative, there is no reason why some other bishop may not be asked, provided the proposed congregation has its intrinsic merit and fulfills a need elsewhere.

The Normae of the Sacred Congregation of Religious demand that the bishop approach the Apostolic See for permission *re adhuc integra.*[49] These words suggest that nothing has been done to form a group into a religious congregation through profesion of the vows or through other means. The decree in no way prevents the founder from gathering disciples, nor their forming a pious society living in common and engaging in works of charity, as long as the members do not wear the garb of religious nor assume any religious name or take vows.[50] In fact reason shows this to be the proper course. A new religious society is not to be founded hastily and without thought, and prudence suggests that some notion be had of the life to be followed which only experience can give. Besides, at least three members must be had for a beginning in order to make up a moral person,[51] and only time and labor and zeal can combine to draw followers in sufficient numbers. Furthermore, the nature and character of the institute should be carefully considered and tested by experience. Many other things must be decided upon, such as the habit, its form, shape,

[48] Laurentius, *Inst. Jur. Eccles.*, p. 580.
[49] *Normae* (1921), n. 3—*A. A. S.*, XIII (1921), 313.
[50] Vermeersch-Creusen, *Epitome*, I, n. 551.
[51] Canon 100, § 2.

color; the constitutions which are to be the spiritual guide of the community; and the means of sustenance without which they can not thrive.

There are certain sections of the *Normae* which the bishop will be wise to heed and to take notice of at this time. There are certain kinds of religious institutes that the Apostolic See circumspectly approves, others again that it never appoves or praises.[52] The *Normae* issued by the Congregation of Religious can in no way be said to be law for the bishop and in the strict sense they are only guides, leaving the bishop free to approve the various kinds of religious institutes which will not be approved by the Holy See. But as a matter of fact, if not obligated by general law, he will be restricted in particular cases if the nature of the work undertaken is such as is repugnant to the religious state. So it will be wise on his part to observe these *Normae,* especially as later on such institutes would find themselves unable to obtain the Holy See's approval. Besides, the decree issued by the Congregation of Religious in 1922 demands that the bishop have before his eyes those things which the *Normae* have decreed for the foundation of religious congregations.[53] Exceptions will be made in individual cases, more easily in favor of missionary countries, and to some extent in those countries which are not strictly Catholic.

Excepting in missionary countries, no congregation will be praised or approved which has not a fixed and proper scope, or which intends to embrace all works of piety and charity each differing entirely from the other.[55] Besides attention is called by the Holy See to certain kinds of communities to which approbation is seldom given. The bishop is admonished to proceed most cautiously in approving institutes which intend to live on alms collected from door to door (n. 14). Nor

[52] *Normae* (1921), cap. II, n. 13-18—*A. A. S.,* XIII (1921), 315.
[53] N. VII—*A. A. S.,* XIV (1922), p. 645.
[54] *Normae* (1921), n. 13.
[55] *Normae* (1921), n. 13.

should he readily approve new religious congregations of sisters, especially with perpetual vows, who propose as their scope to help the infirm of both sexes in their private homes by day and night nursing, or to perform daily domestic service in the homes of the poor.

Neither will approbation be easily conceded to communities of sisters whose special purpose is, (a) to open sanitariums or hotels for persons of both sexes, (b) to establish hospitals for infirm priests, (c) to teach in mixed schools the youth of both sexes (n. 16). And much less will those be approved whose purpose is to care for expectant mothers or to engage in any similar occupations unbecoming the religious state (n. 17). It is never stated, one should note, that these same communities will never be approved, but it is indicated that the Holy See requires extreme care and grave causes as justification of these, and then proper safeguards should be placed as the nature of the individual case demands.

Article 3

The Power of the State

The Church has the right and the duty to promote and foster the expansion and the internal sanctification of all religious institutes. Since these are solely religious societies her right in them is complete and entirely independent of any other society.[56] This principle arises from the conception of the Church as a perfect society, with full power to ordain all things to the end of her creation, the salvation of man through sanctification. This statement does not prescind from the supremacy of the state acting in its own sphere and concerning itself about the temporal welfare of man, but admittedly it proclaims that the state exceeds its authority when it enacts legislation infringing upon the inherent rights of the Church.

[56] Cappello, *Summa Juris Pub. Ecclesiastici*, n. 422, 2°.

It may be enunciated with assurance that the state can not validly erect a religious institute and give it true canonical personality sinces this canonical personality is created solely through ecclesiastical power.[57] Generally, as a matter of fact, the state does not endeavor to do so.[58]

Theoretically, the relationship between the two societies should be one of amity and co-operation. But the Church has seldom found the state willing to co-operate with her and as a result in the past she has been forced to wage bitter struggles to prevent encroachments on her prerogatives. The religious generally have borne the brunt of the attacks from the state which assaults have taken various forms in different ages. Governments have existed which forbade these religious societies to exist or made laws compliance with which spelled a slow but sure extinction for existing institutes.[59] Governmental authorization has been demanded for the foundation of religious congregations and even inspection of the constitutions and particular laws of the religious communities has in many cases been required.[60]

The Church passively tolerates such encroachments precisely to avoid greater evils, realizing that any ignoring of these civil laws would bring about the total dissolution of religious institutes in those countries where these obnoxious laws exist. The right of the state is not thereby recognized but such course is taken unwillingly and only in submission to force. The Church has never ceased to complain of this usurpa-

[57] Canon 100, § 1; Schaefer, *De Rel.*, n. 40 e; Cappello, *op. cit.*, n. 423.

[58] Wernz, *Jus Dec.*, III, n. 611, scholion.

[59] Confer the Sac. Cong. of Bishops and Regulars, *Mariten.*, March 12, 1904—*A. S. S.*, XXXVII, 242; Dubium—*A. S. S.*, XXXIV, 118.

[60] Vermeersch, *De Rel.*, II, n. 140, referring to a response of the Sacred Penitentiary in 1820 regarding Belgian laws. Also the response of the Congregation of Bishops and Regulars regarding French laws—*A. S. S.*, XXXIV, 118. So also we find that the Sisters of the Holy Childhood of Jesus and Mary, whose motherhouse was at Draguignan, received state authorization in 1853—*Cath. Encyc.*, VIII, 374. The action of the state in laying down regulations for religious societies is severely condemned in propositions 52 and 53 of the Syllabus of Pius IX—Denzinger, *Enchiridion*, n. 1752, 1753.

tion and tyranny, and has always upheld the right of these institutes to exist without the permission of the state. The duty of the state is plain. It must recognize only those institutes that the Church has recognized, and these as juridical persons subject entirely to the Church. The state should acknowledge the privileges conferred on these by the Church and permit them also to enjoy the privileges of common law. Besides they should be given a standing in the civil forum and all their rights protected.[61] It follows then that the Church must be free and independent of all civil authority in establishing religious institutes. Due acknowledgment, it is true, must be given to civil laws as far as civil effects are concerned that order be preserved in society. Civil laws, however, which invade and trespass upon the rights of the Church are patently null and void.[62]

To obviate various difficulties which arise in their relations, the Church has recourse to concordats or agreements between a country and herself wherein all matters that may cause friction are settled by compromise.[63] In these agreements references are usually made with regard to the attitude of the state towards religious institutes. The state generally assumes the obligation of recognizing institutes that have been canonically established by proper ecclesiastical authority. Thus in the Concordat with Italy, article 29-b reads: "The juridical status shall be recognized of religious associations, with or without vows which are approved by the Holy See" . . . and article 31: "The creation of new ecclesiastical bodies or religious associations shall be made by ecclesiastical authority in accordance with the rules of canon law and recognition of their juridical status, as far as civil effects are concerned, shall be made by civil authorities."[64] Other states admit the same liberty as existing in ecclesiastical authorities, that is, they allow the foundation of new congregations without interference from the state

[61] Cappello, *Summa Jur. Pub.*, n. 424.
[62] Cappello, *op. cit.*, n. 424 4°.
[63] Augustine, *A Commentary on Canon Law*, I, 223.
[64] Parsons, *The Pope and Italy*, pp. 106, 109.

and also agree to recognize institutes lawfully established. Thus Bavaria in 1925,[65] also Poland,[66] as likewise Lithuania,[67] all treat this point directly and leave the Church free to establish religious communities at will. The Concordat with Prussia does not treat the matter specifically.[68] One of the few countries which restrict the right of the Church, at least if we consider the later concordats, is Rumania which is willing to recognize the already established institutes but demands state permission and that of the Holy See before a new congregation may be founded.[69] This does not mean that the power of the bishop as defined in the Code is taken away but refers to the previous consent of the Holy See which the bishop must always obtain in accordance with the Code.

As can be noticed the period following the war was characterized by numerous concordats. The formation of new countries, the change of regime in some of the old, and also the changing fortunes of other states were greatly influential in causing such agreements. Where no conflicts and disagreements have occurred between the Catholic Church and the state, the state does not concern itself at all with the religious aspect or the foundation of religious congregations, and their growth is as a consequence regulated only by the Church. Such are the conditions which exist in our country and likewise in many others.

---

[65] Art. 2: "Gli Ordini e le Congregazioni religiose possono liberamente fondarsi in conformita delle prozcrizioni canoniche, ne soggiaceiono ad alcuna limitazione da parte dello Stato."—A. A. S., XVII (1925), p. 42, art. 2.

[66] Art. 10—A. A. S., XVII (1925), 277.

[67] Art. 10—A. A. S., XIX (1927), 427.

[68] *A. A. S.*, XXI (1929), 521.

[69] The point is treated specifically in art. 17 and 20, which have: "Aux Ordres et Congrégations religieuses, comme tels, l'Etat reconnait la Personalité juridique, parcequ'ils remplissent les conditions éstablies par les lois en vigeur."

"4°. De nouveaux Ordres et Congrégations réligieuses poutront s'établir en Roumanie et ceux qui y sont actuellement pourront ouvrir des masons nouvelles, seulement avèc l'approbation donnée d'accord par le Saint-Siège et par le Gouvenement Roumain."—*A. A. S.*, XXI (1929), 448.

Article 4

Competence of Roman Congregations

Since the Holy See has considerable to do with the approbation of each new religious community, either through previous consent or later approval, it will not be amiss to understand what is meant by the term Holy See. When the Apostolic See is referred to, it signifies not only the Pope, but also the various congregations, offices, tribunals, which have been created by the Pope in order to take care of matters which pertain to the Holy See.[70]

Up to the thirteenth century and for some time after, it seems as though the Pope did the work of approving new religious institutes personally. At least there was no special body of men appointed to examine the rules of any new religious organization. It is not unreasonable, however, to suppose that in individual cases the Pontiff may have appointed a commission to investigate a proposed new rule. But for a long time after St. Francis no new rule was established, for the Lateran and Lyons Councils had prescribed that new orders adopt one of the older recognized rules. After the Council of Trent, custom for a time seemed to confer the power of examining new constitutions to the Congregation for Interpreting the Decrees of the Council of Trent. The earnest wish of the times was to preserve intact the decrees of this Council and so this Congregation came into being. When examining new constitutions the Congregation's main purpose was to see that nothing was contained in them contrary to the statutes of the Council of Trent. Thus we read that the constitutions of the Anglican Virgins were subjected to examination by this body.[72] When in the nineteenth century a stupendous growth of new religious institutes took place this office was given principally to the Congregation of Bishops and Regulars, al-

[70] Canon 7.

[72] Benedict XIV, Constitution, *Quamvis Justo,* § 2, n. 8—*Fontes*, n. 398; Colomiatti, *Codex Juris Pontificis,* II,. 51.

though the Congregation of the Propagation of the Faith also was competent in its own sphere and approved exclusively for places under its care. Exceptions were made at times and, due to special considerations, this work was given sometimes to the Congregation of the Council or to some special congregation or body created by the Pope for a specific case.[73]

Nowadays after the Code the Congregations that are ordinarily competent are three: the Congregation of Religious, the Congregation of the Propagation of the Faith, and the Congregation for the Orientals. In extraordinary occasions special commissions are sometimes appointed for this work but in that case the rules for their guidance are the special regulations laid down in the decree which grants this power to them. As one of these three Congregations is ordinarily competent, consideration of their history and their present competency is given here.

I. The Congregation of Religious as astablished now owes its existence to the Constitution, *Sapienti consilio,* June, 29, 1908, which constitution reformed and changed the Roman Curia in all its branches.[74] The code left this congregation intact though later on some minor change was made regarding its powers. Historically it traces its origin to the time of Sixtus V who established it by the brief, *Romanus Pontifex,* May 17, 1586.[75] Shortly afterwards one Congregation was formed of what before had been two distinct congregations and became known as the Congregation of Bishops and Regulars. Under this name it survived until the above mentioned constitution of Pius X. To this Congregation belonged as the name implies, all that pertained to the right administration of the diocese and all affairs pertaining to religious. No mention is made of the particular task of approving religious institutes. In fact it is well known that this

[73] Colomiatti, *op. cit.*, II, 156, footnote n. 1.

[74] I, 5°—*A. A. S.*, I (1909), 11.

[75] Bizzarri, *Collectanea*, p. 1; Bouix, *Tractatus de Curia Romana*, 218-219; Ojetti, *Synopsis Rerum Moralium*, n. 3425.

work was not always done by this Congregation. Only in the nineteenth century did the policy become fixed and established as the many examples in Bizzarri show. Furthermore its jurisdiction was limited to so-called Catholic countries where the Church was already firmly established.

The constitution "*Sapienti consilio*" changed this limitation and gave the Congregation authority over all religious as religious in any part of the world. The natural consequence is that it has exclusive right to examine and consider any request for approbation by a religious institute in any part of the world. However, a general exception has been made for Orientals and a few particular exceptions for purely missionary communities. The nature and extent of the power of the Congregation is found in canon 251 of the new Code. Its power, as can be seen from this canon, is most ample as to territory and persons and may be lawfully exercised everywhere. But, by reason of persons its power is restricted not only by the Congregation for the Oriental Church,[76] but also by the Congregation of the Propagation of the Faith.[77] It is thus competent to pass judgment on all religious as such and their communities outside of the exceptions made in favor of the other two Congregations.

II. The second Congregation that enjoys competency is the Congregation of the Propagation of the Faith, the power of which has been very much restricted since 1908. It was most extensive before this date and extended to all institutes in the territory under its jurisdiction. Its origin is traced back to the constitution "Inscrutabili" of Gregory XV, June 22, 1622.[78] It was the last of the greater Congregations to be established by the Holy See, but it soon outshone the others

[76] Canon 257, §1 and § 2.

[77] Canon 252, § 5.

[78] Bouix, *Tractatus de Curia Romana*, Pars II, C. 8, § 1; Peter Guilday, "The Sacred Cong. de Propaganda Fide"—*Catholic Hist. Review*, I (1921), 479; Ojetti, *op. cit.*, n. 3341; Vromant, *Jus Miss.*, n. 5; *Collectania S. Cong. de Prop. Fide*, I, n. 3.

by the magnitude of its power.[79] Its object was to spread the faith in the many new lands that had been discovered about this time and partially also organized reconquest of lands that had been severed from the Church through Protestantism.[80] Its jurisdiction was principally in those regions in which canonically erected dioceses or bishoprics were not in existence.[81] The divisions of territory under its control were administered by Vicars or Delegates of the Holy See.

In the course of time a special commission was established as a part of this Congregation the purpose of which was to examine the constitutions of religious congregations which had their origin in the territory under its control.[82] These were institutes which either had their mother house in the territory subject to the Congregation of the Propaganda or those which by their proper and peculiar scope were destined for the missions.[83] Up to 1908 it exercised this power in many instances and all religious congregations that came under its jurisdiction had to apply to it for approbation.[84] The constitution "*Sapienti consilio*" (1908) changed and limited exceedingly the power of this Congregation over religious as can be seen when referring to I, n. 6, § 5 of this constitution which says:

Quod vero spectat ad sodales religiosos, eadem Congregatio sibi vindicat religiosos qua missionarios, sive uti singulos sive simul sumptos, tangit. Quidquid vero religiosos qua tales,

---

[79] Peter Guilday, "The Sac. Cong. de Prop. Fide"—*Cath. Hist. Review*, I (1921), 479.

[80] U. Benigni, "The Sacred Congregation of Propaganda"—*Cath. Encyc.*, XII, 456.

[81] Bouix, *De Curia Romana*, Pars II, c. 8, § 2.

[82] Ojetti, *Synopsis Rer. Moralium*, n. 3353; Vromant, *Jus Miss.*, n. 12.

[83] Vermeersch, A., *Periodica de Re Can. et Morali*, II (1911), 103.

[84] Many examples could be shown, thus, Colomiatti I (1-3) p. 897 mentions several. Also Vicente, *Inst. Rec.*, n. 51. As a matter of fact all religious communities that started in the United States before 1908 and sought the Holy See's approval obtained it through this Congregation. It was also this Congregation which settled the famous case concerning the nature of the vows of religious orders in the United States. Cf. *A. S. S.*, I, 709.

sive uti singulos sive simul sumptos attingit, ad Congregationem religiosorum negotiis praepositam remittat aut relinquat.[85] This is repeated word for word in the new Code.[86]

From the contents of these words one can easily see that the approval of religious institutes other than those of the Oriental rite is no longer proper to this Congregation. Thus after this promulgation, any new or old community of religious seeking approbation has to apply to the Congregation of Religious even if it arises in a missionary country subject entirely to the Propaganda or even if its scope is purely missionary. For certainly any approval touches religious institutes as religious as the sole purpose of this approval is to pass judgment on the religious life. Later, the Congregation of the Consistory was asked whether those institutes which had already been approved by the Propaganda should come under the power of the Congregation of Religious, and the answer was that they should abide by the constitution *Sapienti consilio*.[87] The prevalent purpose seems to have been to bring about unity of rule for all religious and to have all under one head.[88]

When practically applied, this change of competency in some cases did not produce the best results and special arrangement in particular instances is slowly bringing about a change to the extent that this Congregation is gradually being invested with power over purely missionary institutes, that is, such as have purely missionary activities as their secondary scope. However, one can not say that the law is changed relative to this point, but that particular concessions have been tolerated and allowed by the Holy See.[89] That the power to approve missionary congregations has in some instances been given to the Congregation of the Propagation of the Faith can be seen from its actual approbation of certain missionary institutes. Thus, in 1909, it approved the Congregation of the

[85] *A. A. S.*, I (1909), 11.
[86] Canon 252, § 5.
[87] Vermeersch, A., *Periodica*, IV (1913), n. 308; Ojetti, *op. cit.*, n. 3348.
[88] Vermeersch, A., *Periodica*, IV (1913), n. 308.
[89] Vromant, *Jus Miss.*, p. 12, n. 12.

Missionaries of La Salette.[90] In 1921 the Congregation of the Missionaries of the B. V. M. of Scheut was also placed under this Congregation by a special decree.[92] The same favor has been granted to the institute called Missionaries Canonesses of St. Augustine in Belgium which was approved October 1, 1926.[93]

From these it appears that it will not be long before these exceptions will become more general either by particular laws or by custom. There seems to be no reason why this jurisdiction should not be extended to any community which has for its scope missionary activities in places under the care of the Congregation of the Propagation of the Faith. Yet concessions made thus far are particular concessions and apply only to the cases mentioned, and consequently it can not yet be said that this Congregation has the right to approve all missionary institutes. However, it does seem to be the mind of the Church to grant this power whenever it is sought. Practically, whenever a new institute is to begin or approaches the Holy See in any stage of approbation it should apply to the Congregation of Religious since the law of the Code still holds and has not been abrogated by any contrary custom.[94]

III. The third Congregation competent in any manner to approve religious institutes is the Congregation for the Oriental Church. Indirectly it may be considered an outgrowth of the previous Congregation since one of its main purposes was to bring back the Schismatics to the unity of the faith.[95] In general the duty that it now performs was done by the Propaganda, which at times had a special commission as part

[90] *A. A. S.*, I (1909), 233.
[92] *A. A. S.*, XIII (1921), 354.
[93] Vromant, *op. cit.*, p. 13, footnote n. 1.
[94] Societies, not strictly religious, because they have but one vow or because of some other deficiency, are subject to the Propaganda, if they are purely missionary in scope. This is by general law as they are not truly religious. Cf. Vermeersch, *Periodica, V*, n. 391; *Comm. Pro. Rel.*, II (1921), 125.
[95] Ojetti, *op. cit.*, n. 3341.

of itself, which was to handle Oriental affairs.[96] It was however on June 6, 1862, that Pious IX in his constitution *Romani pontificis* established a separate commission for Oriental affairs, having the prefect of the Propaganda as its head, but having its own secretary, consultors, and official interpreters.[97] The Vatican Council kept this division also. Cf. *Collect. Lac.* VII, c. 847. The constitution "*Sapienti consilio*" did not change this separate commission but retained it as a special part of the Propaganda and preserved for it all the rights it had possessed previously. Its power to approve at this time is shown by its action in approving the constitutions of the Armenian Mechitaristae in 1909.[98] Its right to approve religious communities of the Oriental Rite was not lost by the constitution of Pius X, "*Sapienti consilio*".[99] As a special body entirely independent it came into existence through the *Motu Proprio* of Benedict XV, *Dei providentis* of May 1, 1917.[100] The Code did not change this and consequently its competency now extends to all of whatever nature pertains to the persons, the discipline or the rite of the Oriental Church.[101] It has power then to approve religious institutes whose members belong to the Oriental Rite and those Oriental religious who desire the Supreme Pontiff's seal of approbation can only obtain it through this Congregation.

These are the ordinary instruments of the Holy See for approving religious institutes, and usually the work is done by one of these according to the law. The Pope has acted differently at times and may do so in the future, as at times it has happened that approbation was given by one of the Roman Offices, or by the Secretary of State, or by the

---

96 This commission as part of the Propaganda confirmed the constitutions of the Congregation of Mt. Lebanon of the Syrian Maronite Monks of the Order of St. Anthony in 1732. Various others also could be mentioned. Cf. Colomiatti, *Codex Juris Pontif.* I, (1-3), p. 884.

97 Wernz-Vidal, *Jus Canonicum* II, n. 500; Ojetti, *op. cit.*, n. 3350.

98 *A. A. S.*, I (1909), 704.

99 Vermeersch, *Periodica*, IV, n. 308.

100 *A. A. S.*, IX (1917), 529; Wernz-Vidal, *op. cit.*, II, n. 500.

101 Canon 257.

Apostolic Chancellor.[103] Then again a particular commission of cardinals may be appointed for a particular instance. These, however, are all in the nature of exceptions and so may be called extraordinary methods of approval. In the majority of cases one of the three above mentioned congregations is given the task. There is nothing though to forbid or prevent a community's approaching the Pope directly but it is hardly probable that he would personally consider such a request because of the great loss of time that it would entail for him.

---

[103] *Comm. Pro Rel.*, II (1921), 282; Schaefer, *De Rel.*, n. 41, footnote n. 2.

CHAPTER IV.

A COMMENTARY ON CANON 492.

ARTICLE I.

Can. 492, § 1. *Episcopi, non autem Vicarius Capitularis vel Vicarius Generalis, condere possunt Congregationes religiosas; sed eas ne condant neve condi sinant, inconsulta Sede Apostolica; quod si agatur de tertiariis in communi viventibus, requiritur praeterea ut a supremo Moderatore primi Ordinis suae religioni aggregentur.*

These words express the law as it now stands. The canon is but a repetition in substance of the law that existed for some time, as confirmed by Leo XIII and modified by Pius X. The concession of this power to the bishop is influenced by the constitution "*Conditae a Christo*" of Leo XIII, whereas the necessity of consulting the Holy See is found in the Motu proprio "*Dei providentis*" of Pius X. The explicit denial of this power to the Vicar General and Vicar Capitular is new entirely and is not to be found in any of the older laws. The reasons for this exclusion will be apparent in the commentary on that section. Thus in general it can truly be said that no new law is found here, but rather a restatement of old legislation which had been in force for some time.

I. *Episcopi.* It is but proper that this power should be entrusted to the care of the bishop as he is the ordinary and immediate pastor of the diocese allotted to him by the Holy See.[1] He is subject to no one but the Pope who, however, can

[1] Augustine, *Rights and Duties of Ordinaries*, p. 49.

limit a bishop's power in a certain sense especially as to the ecclesiastical jurisdiction which he receives from the Supreme Pontiff.[2] Ordinarily this power belongs to the bishop and only through necessity was the Pope in past ages obliged to withdraw this power temporarily, as history shows. As pastor the bishop must seek to sanctify souls and an obligation is imposed upon him by divine law to encourage this higher life of sanctity in his subjects.

The term *bishop* is used here only in reference to residential bishops and so titular bishops would not be included, for in law unless the contrary is said or it is otherwise apparent from the nature of the thing, the word *episcopus* refers only to residential bishops, not titular. When the Code wishes to include the latter it mentions them explicitly.[3] By residential bishops are meant those placed in charge of a diocese according to the regulations of canon law. For the valid use of his power of jurisdiction according to positive law depends upon his having obtained canonical possession of the office, and before such possession no act of jurisdiction is valid.[4] A bishop need not, however, wait until his consecration for this possession but may properly present his credentials any time after his appointment and so receive the power of jurisdiction before his consecration.[5]

Wherever a diocese is canonically erected a bishop is ordinarily in charge and to him this power is given by virtue of the canon under consideration. Yet there are other persons whose office is similar to that of the bishop and who therefore are included under this name. For, granted the episcopal power may not be theirs, their work is similar to that of the bishop and so they are included under the name of bishop unless the

---

[2] Wernz-Vidal, *De Personis*, II, n. 609.

[3] Larraona, "Commentarium Codicis", *Comm. pro Rel.*, IV (1923), 109; cf. Canons 223, § 2; 348; 349, § 1, etc.

[4] Canon 334, § 2; Vermeersch-Creusen, *Epitome*, I, n. 404; Wernz-Vidal, *De Personis*, II, n. 597, n. 2.

[5] Canon 334, § 3; Wernz-Vidal, *op. cit.*, II, n. 597; Augustine, *Rights and Duties of Ordinaries*, p. 13.

nature of the thing or the context should prevent their inclusion. There is no reason given here to lead us to suppose that these same persons are excluded.

Those then included besides the bishop are Abbots or prelates *Nullius* who preside over a territory which is not included in any diocese.[6] The reason is because they too have the care of souls the same as bishops. For the same reason this power is also given to permanent Apostolic Administrators, who for weighty and special reasons are appointed by the Holy See in exceptional cases over a canonically erected diocese.[7] This position is only given when the precarious conditions of the diocese warrant such action on the part of the Pope; or else in time of political trouble,[8] or because of some fault on the part of the bishop.[9] When permanently established, Apostolic Administrators have the same rights as the bishop,[10] and thus they possess the capacity to approve religious congregations.[11] If, on the contrary, his office were temporary, then this power would not be conferred on him as then his rights are similar to the Vicar Capitular's and the right to approve is denied to the latter explicitly in this canon.[12]

Apostolic Vicars and Prefects, ruling in a territory which has not yet been erected into a diocese, have the same power also as residential bishops and hence are also given the power by this canon to establish religious congregations.[13] All the above mentioned can do this by virtue of the ordinary power which they possess,[14] and once duly installed may do it through the concession of this canon without the necessity of obtaining special power from Rome.

[6] Canon 215, § 2; 323, § 1; Schaefer, De Rel., n. 70; Larraona, *Commentarium Codicis—Comm. pro Rel.* V (1924), 42.

[7] Canon 312.

[8] Augustine, *A Commentary on Canon Law*, II, 326.

[9] Wernz-Vidal, *De Personis*, II, n. 557.

[10] Canon 315, § 1.

[11] Larraona, *Commentarium Codicis—Comm. pro Rel.*, V (1924), 42; Schaefer, *op. cit.*, n. 70.

[12] Canon 315, § 2, 1°.

[13] Canon 294, § 1.

[14] Schaefer, *De Relig.*, n. 70.

Since all possess this faculty by virtue of their office it must be conceded that it is ordinary power in the sense of canon 197, §1. Therefore this power can and may be delegated according to canon 199, §1, either generally or in particular cases.[15] No particular reason can be adduced to show the invalidity of such delegation, nor the illiceity, though it must be admitted that it would be inexpedient for the bishop to give a general delegation, since this is considered a matter of the greatest importance which should, under ordinary circumstances, be in charge of the bishop.

II. *Non autem Vicarius Capitularis vel Vicarius Generalis.* Both are mentioned particularly as excluded because if not explicitly mentioned they also would possess the power the same as bishops.[16] The Vicar Capitular's office is temporary and lasts only for the time the office is vacant until a successor legitimately takes possession. It is not proper that he do anything of grave and serious importance which would materially change conditions in the diocese, and such would be effected through the foundation of a new religious community. The desire of the Code when a vacancy occurs is plainly expressed in these words, *Sede vacante nihil innovetur.*[17] A new religious community is considered a great change in the eyes of the Code and for this reason this power is especially withdrawn from the Vicar Capitular by general law.

From canon 368 it is seen that the Vicar General participates in the jurisdiction of the bishop, and his jurisdiction is the same in scope over the whole diocese, though it be vicarious. Thus he has power in spiritual and temporal affairs except: first, in those cases which are reserved by the Ordinary, and sceondly, in those which by law require a special mandate from the bishop. He is excluded by name in this canon because if

[15] Larraona, "Commentarium Codicis"—*Comm. pro Rel.*, V (1924), 42.

[16] Canons 435, § 1; 368, § 1. Ayrinhac, *Constitution of the Church in the New Code of Canon Law,* II, n. 221, p. 275.

[17] Canon 436.

not mentioned explicitly as lacking this power he would possess it by his ordinary power. The reason for denying him this faculty is the same as that assigned above when speaking of the Vicar Capitular.

An interesting question may be brought out here though it is not of much practical value. Usually when the law restricts the power of the Vicar General it says, "unless he have a special mandate from the bishop," or other similar words.[18] In this canon nothing is said of a special mandate. Could the bishop give him a special mandate for all cases and so permit the Vicar General to found religious communities through his ordinary power? Some authors say that even if he were endowed with a special mandate the Vicar General would have no authority to make such foundations.[19] The reason seems to be that certain negotiations are of such moment that they are excluded from the limits of a special mandate and undoubtedly the erection of a new community is a matter of the highest importance.[20] Schaefer admits the possibility of a special mandate.[21] Practically it makes little difference since he can be delegated for all cases. If approbation is given by one who has delegated power or is not entitled to give it by general law, it would be better to mention in the decree of erection the origin of the power so that later no doubt may arise as to the validity of the erection.

It is logical to conclude that other inferior superiors are not of their own power and office entitled to found religious institutes. Major Superiors of exempt religious communities, though Ordinaries in the sense of the Code, do not enjoy this prerogative as they are not included under the term "bishop," which is equivalent to the Ordinary of the place.[22] The Cardi-

---

[18] Cf. Canons 113, 152, 357, § 1.

[19] Augustine, *A Commentary on Canon Law*, III, 65; Larraona, *Comm. pro Rel.*, V (1924), 43; Toso, *De Personis*, L. II, P. II, *De Rel.*, p. 14.

[20] Toso, *De Religiosis*, p. 14.

[21] Schaefer, *De Religiosis*, n. 70.

[22] Schaefer, *op. cit.*, n. 70.

nal Vicar of Rome, whose office is somewhat similar to that of the Vicar General, by particular law has jurisdiction similar to a bishop's and so has ordinary power to establish religious communities.[23]

If, then, any other than legitimate authority approve, such an act surely would be invalid because no legal personality can be conferred except through competent ecclesiastical authority.[24] Furthermore, according to the canonical definition, no institute can become a religious congregation unless the proper authority brings it into being.[25] Any power, other than ecclesiastical, would of its nature be totally incompetent. It is needless to say that the Pope is not limited in any way by this canon and he can at will establish a religious congregation anywhere in the world since his power is in nowise limited here on earth.

Implicitly there is a grave prohibition upon all the faithful not to attempt to establish religious life on a new basis without authorization of some one empowered by the Church to give permission. For the Church alone is the proper judge as to the fitness, utility and practical value for sanctification of any mode of life that may be thought out, and submission to Holy Mother Church and faithful attention to her advice should be the outstanding traits of all the founders of religious institutes.

III. *Condere Possunt.* The Ordinary of the place and all those who have equivalent power as we have seen above are permitted by law to establish religious congregations. The word *condere* here means to build, found, establish, and according to the norm of law is an act of a legitimate superior granting juridical personality to a group of faithful who are desirous of professing religious life.[26] It is entirely a new creation, the beginning of a new institute in the strictest sense of

[23] Larraona, *Comm. pro Rel.*, V (1924), 45.
[24] Canon 100, § 1.
[25] Canon 488.
[26] Larraona, *Comm. pro Rel.*, V (1924), 45.

the term. By this act the group is changed from a private group of individuals to a public society in the Church with all the rights consequent upon this elevation.

To erect, then, is here synonymous with approval. For to give a number of persons permission to establish a religious society and to allow them publicly to profess this life is an indication that the bishop approves their mode of living. And so joined with this act of erection is an act of his ecclesiastical power whereby the bishop judges this life not only to be useful, but also conducive to perfection for those professing it. In this sense the erection of a religious congregation is called approbation. It follows that such foundation should only be permitted after a thorough investigation of the motives, habits and life of the founder, and also after a knowledge of the nature and special characteristics of the institute to be created. For approbation can follow only when all the notes and attributes of a thing are fully known. This is a grave obligation placed upon the bishop by the Holy See and also by conscience. The bishop must investigate beforehand so that when he gives his consent to the erection it will be an approbation in the full sense of the word.

The principal effect of the episcopal approbation is the formation of a society into an ecclesiastical moral person, both collegiate and non-collegiate.[27] The society is publicly acknowledged as belonging to the religious state and consequently enjoys all the rights of the religious state according to its status as a diocesan religious community. Though according to paragraph two of this canon the society remains subject to the bishop according to the norm of law, yet it can have its own internal regime, as a society, and also its internal authority for the affairs which pertain to it as a society.[28] The particular

[27] Canon 99. It is useful to note here also that as such, a religious community can not begin with less than three persons since the Code states a moral person can not be created except it have at least three physical persons. Cf. Canon 100, § 2. This law is laid down for the validity of the act. Toso, *Commentaria Minora*, Lib. II, pars II, p. 41.

[28] Schaefer, *De Religiosis*, n. 71.

laws, however, which are to be used in governing the society, are to be made at the discretion of the bishop and these he may change or amend as he sees fit except those points which have already been submitted to the Holy See.

The Code is silent about the manner of erection. In speaking of moral persons in general it decrees that the erection be done by formal decree.[29] Before the new law it was certain that no formal decree was required, and thus any approbation or permission sufficed no matter how granted.[30] Furthermore, it does not seem certain that such formal decree in writing is required by the Code, since religious houses and provinces and also institutes apparently can be legitimately established in any way.[31] However, in order to remove all doubts as to the legitimate existence of new religious communities, the Congregation of Religious issued a decree in 1922 demanding that the establishment of new institutes hereafter be only by formal decree and in writing. After definitely treating of the uncertainties of erections before the Code and after duly providing for whatever was necessary to give these institutes legitimate and valid existence it lays down certain laws for the future. It decrees that henceforth whenever the Ordinary wishes to erect any new religious congregation or pious society, he should do this by formal decree and in writing, an exemplar of which should be kept by the community and besides in the archives of the diocese. After the establishment, a copy should also be sent to the Congregation of Religious.[32] Towards the close of

---

[29] Canon 100, § 1.

[30] Larraona, *Comm. pro Rel.*, IV (1923), 199; Schaefer, *op. cit.*, n. 69.

[31] Larraona, *Comm. pro Rel.*, IV (1923), 199; Schaefer, *op. cit.*, n. 69.

[32] Thus in n. VII of the document it is stated: "In posterum vero, quatenus Ordinarius, debita venia Apostolicae Sedis obtenta, aliquam novam Congregationem aut Piam societatem religiosam erigere voluerit, satagat ut erectio fiat per formale decretum in scriptis datum, cuius exemplar tam in tabulario Instituti quam in Archivo diocesano servandum erit. De peracta autem huiusmodi erectione hanc Sacram Congregationem edoceat, ac decreti examplar transmittat, in quo praecipue curet ut tam titulus quam scopus Instituti peculiaris explicite et exacte praefiniatur, habitis prae oculis iis quae de hac in *Normis*, a Sacra Congregatione appro-

this decree it is stated that the decree was approved by His Holiness who ordered that in the future it should be observed by all.

This decree does not change the nature of the act, nor does it cause a neglect of its observance to invalidate the act of approval. The reason is apparent, for though the decree is obligatory, yet in no way is it insinuated that the bishop's decree must be in writing in order that the foundation be valid. There are several reasons for the decree, but the chief are these: first, there was never any assurance of legal existence; second, the existence of many was not known by the Holy See; and third, it is unbecoming that the number of institutes be concealed from Rome since later they must transact business with the Apostolic See.[33] The chief purpose though is to avoid all doubt as to the valid erection and also to remove all uncertainties in the future. Thus a certain proof will be had at all times to prove the legitimate and valid existence of a religious community. Before the law a formal document is the best and surest proof.

The nature of a formal document of this kind demands that the name of the person erecting be expressed, that the name of the moral person to be constituted be also mentioned, and the actual act of erecting be expressed by the words, "I erect," "establish," or some similar words. There is no necessity to say explicitly, "I erect into a moral person."[34]

Other things are required which, if absent, make a formal document valueless, such as the date and signature. A signature to be valid should be in one's own handwriting and not typed. Clarity demands further that the place of issue be given, that the full name of the institute and the place of the motherhouse be expressed together with other characteristics

batis sub die 6 martii 1921, cap. II et IV (*Act. Ap. Sedis*, vol. XIII, p. 312), habentur."—Decree of S. Cong. of Rel., *Quod Iam*, November 30, 1922—*A. A. S.*, XIV (1922), 645-646.

[33] Maroto, "Acta et Documenta", *Comm. pro Rel.*, IV (1923), 196.

[34] Vromant, *Jus Miss.*, n. 377.

of note which may help to identify the institute. That the Holy See's permission has been obtained ought also to be mentioned.

The law does not state what else should appear on the written document. It does tell what is desired on the document which is sent to Rome, namely the title and scope of the Institute. And as this document is to be an exemplar of the decree of erection, those two points ought likewise to be on this document. According to this decree of the Sacred Congregation of Religious three copies are necessary, one to be kept in the archives of the institute, the other to be preserved in the diocesan archives, and the third to be transmitted to Rome after the formal act of erection. The reason for this is that there be constant proof in the hands of the authorities interested.

Much importance is placed upon documents in the eyes of the Church, and so they should be made up with a view to their preservation. Durable ink should be employed and only parchment of the best kind. The document ought to be written by hand for then the probabilities of permanency are multiplied. The seal of the bishop adds force to the signature and both combined exclude all reasonable doubt as to the genuineness of the document.

As far as the state is concerned the act of the bishop does not give the institute any civil personality. In the eyes of the state a minor ecclesiastical moral person, not an essential part of a religious denomination, does not exist as a moral person unless so constituted by positive act of the state.[85] Before the civil courts of the state, religious congregations do not form an intergal part of the Catholic religion and so a special act of the civil power is needed to make them moral persons in the eyes of the state. The Church tolerates this in order to protect her own interests, and it is her wish that religious congregations be incorporated according to civil laws, so that they may

[85] Schweiger, "Condicio Religiosorum in Bavaria"—*Comm. pro Rel.*, VI (1925), 366; Toso, *Commentaria Minora*, lib. II, pars II, p. 39.

obtain the protection and privileges of state laws. Besides, in many instances this is the only way that the rights of the religious community can be protected through the state. As to the methods of incorporation these differ in various states and countries and so, before incorporating, the legal advice of one conversant with all the technicalities of the local civil law should be sought.

IV. *Congregationes Religiosas.* The Code tells us plainly what it means by religious congregations when it describes them as institutes whose members make profession of simple vows only, whether perpetual or temporary.[36] By an institute (*religio*) is meant, "Every society, approved by legitimate authority, the members of which tend to evangelical perfection, according to the laws proper to their society, by the profession of public vows, whether perpetual or temporary, the latter renewable after the lapse of a fixed time."[37]

Before the Code the word *religio*, influenced mainly by Benedict XIV[38] was applied solely to institutes with solemn vows.[39] The Code has done away with this distinction and acknowledges all religious congregations as true religious, even if their vows are only temporary.[40] It is a final acknowledgment of the wonderful work these congregations have done in the Church, that they are finally admitted to be true religious and so all the canons of the Code pertaining to religious apply also to them. In interpreting the word *religious* here it must be applied in the strict sense, according to the definition of canon 488, 1° considered together with canon 487. If then any of the notes given in his quasi-canonical definition are lacking in any

[36] Canon 488, 2°.

[37] Canon 488, 1°.

[38] Constitution, *"Quamvis iusto,"* § 13, April 30, 1749—*Fontes*, n. 398; Bouix, *De Reg.*, I, 340.

[39] Vermeersch-Creusen, *Epitome*, I, n. 589.

[40] The framers of the Code hesitated in making this last concession as one can see from the Schema of the Code which was sent out in 1913. Canon 369, § 2 of this Schema had: "---extensive religionis vocabulum comprehendit quoque societatem, legitima auctoritate ecclesiastica approbatam, in qua tria illa vota nonnisi ad tempus nuncupantur."

community, such would not come under consideration here. Hence if a society has only one vow, or two at the most, it would not come under the meaning of this canon as it is not properly a religious institute.[41]

It should be especially noticed in this definition that ecclesiastical approbation is required and the deficiency of this approbation would be such that a society could not be called a religious congregation. Neither is the solitary life here included. There is included here solely a society, having a common life and its own set of particular laws, approved by a legitimate ecclesiastical authority, professing the three vows of poverty, chastity and obedience. The three vows are the minimum. This number would not restrict a community to only three, though at present the Holy See does not view with favor any additional vows besides the three customary ones.[42] It matters little whether the vows are simple or solemn, temporary or perpetual, whether the institute is of pontifical or diocesan right; all come under the heading of religious institutes.[43]

It should be noticed that the Code uses the words *congregationes religiosas* and not *religiones* in canon 492. If the latter term had been used the bishop now would also have the power to establish new orders since at this time the term *religio* is common to both orders and congregations. Orders and congregations differ solely by reason of the vows taken and their effects. These vows have the same form, and the same force of obligation both as to time and persons. But they differ entirely as to their effects; for simple vows make contrary acts illicit, whereas solemn vows make these acts in-

[41] Canon 673. Thus the Lazarists, Sulpicians, and Oratorians of St. Philip Neri are not religious congregations because they do not make profession of the three customary vows. Cf. Vermeersch-Creusen, *Epitome*, I, n. 770; Vicente, *Instit. Rec.*, n. 32. These are often called ecclesiastical or secular congregations. The Code calls them *societates sive virorum sive mulierum in communi viventium sine votis.* Can. 673.

[42] *Normae* (1901), n. 102.

[43] Larraona, "Commentarium Codicis", *Comm. pro Rel.*, IV (1923), 10.

valid at least as far as the act itself can be invalidated.[44] One may say that the Church wishes to give to the former less firmness and stability, whereas the latter have an almost irrevocable character.[45] Authors differ, however, as to the nature of the solemnity of the vows as they have differed from the time of St. Thomas.[46]

This power of approval granted explicitly for the founding of new congregations, does not include the faculty to approve new orders. For all authors agree that the bishop can not validly institute a new order.[47] The Code makes no explict statement, though indirectly it denies the bishop this power. From the IV Lateran Council to this day an unbroken line of witnesses testify to the necessity of papal approbation for an order. The chief reason given today for the reservation to the Pope alone is that the establishment of an order is considered a *Causa major*, which, by custom and practice, is now reserved to the Holy See.

It is difficult to say that the law of the Lateran Council still holds because that law was merely disciplinary and canon 6, 6° thereby abrogates it. What seems to be the real foundation of the present law rests on this law of the Lateran Council which had such influence that, after its decree the power of approving an order was reserved to the Pope alone. In time this power of approving orders was considered to be of so great moment that the right belonged exclusively to the Holy See. And it is considered in the same light today. A *Causa Major* is a negotiation of greater moment which is reserved,

[44] Canon 579; Toso, Commentaria Minora, *De Religiosis*, p. 8.

[45] Decree of S. Cong. of Rel., "*Sacrosancta Dei*," January 1, 1911—*A. A. S.*, III (1911), 29.

[46] St. Thomas, 2, 2, q. 88, art. 7, ad 1; Pejska, *Jus Can. Religiosorum*, p. 9; Vicente, *op. cit.*, n. 11; Bouix, *De Regul.*, I, 68.

[47] Larraona, *Comm. pro Rel.*, V (1924), 44; Fanfani, *De Jure Religiosorum*. p. 7; Vermeersch-Creusen, *Epitome*, I, n. 551; Schaefer, *De Rel.*, n. 63.

either by its very nature or by positive law, to the Holy See.[48] The establishment of an order is of such great importance that it is reserved by its very nature to the Pope.[49]

But other arguments are advanced to show that this power can not be validly exercised by the bishops. If, in order to establish a house of an order the approval of the Holy See is necessary,[50] *a fortiori* the permission of Rome is demanded for the foundation of an order. Besides only the Holy See can establish a diriment impediment as regards matrimony,[51] and by reason of canon 1073 solemn vows which are essential to an order have this invalidating effect. Furthermore, solemn vows are only those that have been so acknowledged by the Church.[52] Also with these solemn vows there exists the privilege of exemption, and only the Holy See can exempt.[53] Likewise solemn vows induce such a bond on the part of the recipient and the Church, so absolute, perpetual and irrevocable, that the bishop is incapable of effecting this.[54] All these reasons, in whole and in part, have led all commentators after the Code to declare no other than the Pope and General Council competent to bring a new religious order into existence.

The *Schema* of the Code, sent out in 1913 to the bishops of the world in order to obtain their opinion, proposed the following legislation about orders: *Ad Sedem Apostolicam tantummodo spectat institutio seu erectio novi Ordinis vel Congregationis regularis.*[55] But the Code as finally promulgated omitted all direct reference to the establishment of new religious orders. The reason for the omission may be said to be practical, in this

[48] Canon 220; Wernz-Vidal, *De Personis,* II n. 429.

[49] Schaefer, *op. cit.,* n. 63; Wernz-Vidal, *De Personis,* II, n. 434.

[50] Canon 497, § 1.

[51] Canon 1039, § 2; Pejska, *Jus Can. Rel.,* p. 14.

[52] Canon 1308, § 2.

[53] Pejska, *op. cit.,* p. 14. It was declared officially before the new Code that the bishop could not solemnize vows. Cf. Sac. Cong. of Bish. & Reg.—*In Aesina Votorum,* December 16, 1863—*A. S. S.,* I, 720; Bizzari, *Collectanea,* 77.

[54] Suarez, *De Rel.,* III, L. II, c. 17, n. 26.

[55] Canon 372, § 1.

that no new order has been established in the Church for the last 150 years and there are no indications that the immediate future will bring any into existence.[56] Some congregations have sought this privilege in the past but for many reasons the Apostolic See has been unwilling to grant it, and at present this frame of mind remains unchanged.[57]

It does happen at times that the Church permits institutes, which by their rule should profess solemnly, yet because of civil laws have not been able to profess solemn vows in the past, to reassume solemn vows whenever and wherever the objections of the state have been lifted.[58] It also can happen, as has happened before, that the Church will raise a congregation to the status of an order. In fact, if the Church institutes any new orders in the future, most likely she will follow this mode of procedure. She can raise an institute to an order immediately but an act of that kind is contrary to the custom of the last two centuries.[59]

V. *Sed eas ne condant neve condi sinant, inconsulta Sede Apostolica.* These words, with the prohibition they contain, had their origin in the *Motu proprio*, "*Dei providentis*" of Pius X.[60] Thereby the Supreme Pontiff made it obligatory for the bishop to consult the Holy See before founding a new community of religious. The reason for the law is to provide for the moderate and proper use of this faculty, lest religious institutes be multiplied without reason. Though Leo XIII had set certain norms as a guide for bishops, Pius X thought that these were not observed sufficiently and that they were in some respects deficient. The Holy See was unwilling to forbid new

[56] The last order approved was in 1752, Ordo Fratrum Poenitentiae by Pius VI, in a brief *Ex debito*—Schaefer, De Rel., n. 64.

[57] Larraona, *Comm. pro Rel.*, I (1920), 138, n. 12.

[58] S. Cong. of Rel., decree, "*Religiosae sanctimonialium*," June 23, 1923—*A. A. S.*, XV (1923), 357-358. The Holy See indicates in this decree that there is nothing to prevent the nuns of France from going back to solemn vows which they formerly professed, provided its permission has been obtained.

[59] Laurentius, *Inst. Jur. Ecc.*, p. 580.

[60] July 16, 1906—*Fontes*, n. 675.

religious congregations entirely, neither did she desire to take the power of establishing them away from the bishops. So a middle course was adhered to thus permitting their growth through the bishops, yet demanding that the latter consult the Holy See first. This measure was found to be practical and so was incorporated into the present law.[61] Because of this law, the Holy See must be consulted before the bishop founds a new community or before he permits another to establish a religious congregation.

This power is granted to the bishops with the stipulation that they, before using it, first consult the See of St. Peter. Nevertheless a foundation without the previous permission of the Holy See would not be invalid, but merely illicit.[62] There is no invalidating clause in this law or the old, nor any hint that any illegal foundation of this sort would be invalid. Because the bishop acts by ordinary power his illicit act would not be invalid, neither would a delegated person's act be invalid provided he were properly authorized.[63] Besides it is stated in canon 11 that those laws only are invalidating when the law expressly or equivalently states so, which surely it does not do here. Were it advisable, the Pope could annul the bishop's act, but generally he does not take recourse to such extreme. Yet even this annulment would not be retroactive, as the validity of the act would be sustained until notice of invalidation.[64]

When should the Holy See be consulted or approached? The *Normae* of 1921 are clear in their answer. In n. 3 of these *Normae* it is stated:

---

[61] Larraona, *Comm. pro Rel.*, V (1924), 46.

[62] Schaefer, *De Rel.*, n. 69; Pejska, *Jus Can. Rel.*, p. 15; Larraona, *Comm. pro Rel.*, V (1924), 48; Toso, *Commentaria Minora*, Lib. II, Pars II, p. 14.

[63] Canon 203, § 1. Canon 105, 2°, has no application here as it speaks of the necessity of a superior to consult an inferior body and not of the obligation of an inferior to consult a superior.

[64] Canon 10.

Quoties aliquis Episcopus, . . .novam religiosam votorum simplicium Congregationem condere opportunum judicaverit re adhuc integra Sacram Congregationem de Religiosis adeat. . . .[65] The words *re adhuc integra* are important. They signify that nothing should be done to form a group into a religious congregation before the Holy See has spoken. The Apostolic See wants to be entirely free to say no or yes to the request of the bishop and so does not want him to do anything that would hamper this freedom. The members of the new society should not be permitted to take vows as religious, though a common life as a trial and test of vocation would not be prohibited before this request to the Sacred Congregation, in fact these are strongly recommended and advisable.[66] There is nothing to prevent the founder from gathering disciples, nor these persons from forming a pious society living in common, nor from engaging in works of charity, as long as the members do not wear the garb of religious or assume any religious name, or take the vows.

Once permission is given there is no reason why the bishop should not proceed to the erection of the religious congregation. As can be seen from the Normae,[67] no obligation rests upon the bishop to erect after the Holy See has given consent to his request. It is merely a permission that the Holy See extends and not a command. And what is more, the actual foundation is made by the bishop, not by the Holy See. He is the one who must judge as to the opportuneness, fitness and

[65] *A. A. S.*, XIII (1921), 319. These *Normae* are law for the Congregation of Religious as they were approved by Benedict XV with the intention to make them obligatory for this Congregation. They do not consequently apply in those cases where the Congregation of the Propaganda or of the Orientals must be approached. The far greater number of cases fall under the jurisdiction of the Congregation of Religious. Besides this is the only body that has made known its regulations. So when the *Normae* are spoken of, both those of 1901 and those of 1921, it should be remembered that they pertain only to those religious congregations that fall under the competency of the Sacred Congregation of Religious. Though where possible it is highly probable that the other Congregations will follow the same norms.

[66] Vermeersch-Creusen, *Epitome,* I, n. 551.

[67] *Normae,* n. 3—A. A. S., XIII (1921), 313.

other qualities of the future congregation and the Apostolic See by consenting only confirms his judgment. Morally it is necessary that he have some solid reasons for refusing after having given his promise; and juridically these persons could have recourse to the Holy See if any injustice had been done to them. Whether the bishop erects or refrains from doing so, in both instances he should make a report to the Holy See, at least that seems to be the tenor of the decree of the Sacred Congregation of Religious in 1922.[68]

If the Sacred Congregation should refuse to accede to the bishop's request, and refuse to permit the new foundation the bishop could nevertheless validly establish. Such refusal would not be a withdrawal of the bishop's power, and, though gravely illicit, his act would be valid. Larraona[69] is of the opinion that the bishop could not validly found under such conditions but ascribes no reason for his statement.

The new *Normae* tell plainly what should be in the letter which is sent by the bishop to the Holy See.[70] The bishop must declare who is the founder of the new institute and give an indication of the founder's character and the reasons that actuate him in his desire. The name or the title of the new institute should also be indicated, and likewise the form, color and material of the habit to be worn by the professed and the novices. He must tell how many and what kind of works the members of the congregation are to assume and by what means they intend to support themselves. In the report he must also mention whether any similar congregations exist in his diocese and what works they do.

All this is mentioned explicitly by the decree but the Sacred Congregation does not say that is all which is required. It desires to know all data necessary for a clear judgment of the opportuneness, the worthiness and all other characteristics of

[68] S. Cong. of Rel., decree, *Quod iam*, November 30, 1922—A. A. S., XIV, (1922), 646.

[69] *Comm. pro Rel.*, V (1924), 48.

[70] *Normae* (1921), n. 4—A. A. S., XIII (1921), 313.

note. Consequently any serious departure from the various norms laid down must be mentioned in order to obtain the permission of the Holy See and to avoid trouble later on when application is made for Papal approbation. Those things that the Sacred Congregation approves, namely the title, name, habit, etc., can not later be changed by the bishop. Constant tradition and the invariable practice of the Roman Curia are unanimous in asserting this,[71] and authors generally agree.[72] The *Normae* are silent, but Pius X had already insisted on this point,[73] and the Code re-asserts it in such manner as to leave no doubt.[74]

Thus it can be said that restrictions placed upon the bishop arise from a twofold source; first, by the Code since he must first consult the Holy See; secondly, by the *Normae* of 1921, the injunctions of which he must follow. In case any special regulations are given by the Holy See he would be obliged to observe these also. Whatever has been submitted to the Holy See can no longer be changed by the bishop.

VI. *Quod si agatur de tertiariis in communi viventibus requiritur praeterea ut a supremo Moderatore primi Ordinis suae religioni aggregentur.* All that has been said in this canon thus far applies also to Tertiaries. The bishop approves them, as any other religious congregation but the Holy See must be consulted. But in order that the new community might be affiliated to the first order it must obtain the consent of the Supreme Moderator of that first order. This refers to Tertiaries living in common and no consideration is given here to third orders secular.

The original purpose of the Third Order which was popularized by St. Francis was for those living at home in the

[71] Benedict XIV, *De Synod. Dioecesana,* I, L. IX, c. 1, n. 6.
[72] Vicente, *Inst. Rec.*, n. 64, p. 31; Larraona, *Comm. pro Rel.,* V (1924), 49; Pejska, *Jus Can. Rel.,* p. 15.
[73] Motu Proprio, *"Dei providentis,"* n. 3—Fontes, 675.
[74] Canon 495, § 2.

world.[75] In time it happened that there were pious women who desired to live in community life and follow the third order rule and still not be shut off from charitable labors. Pius V directed all his energies to change the nature of these institutes of the third order but he did not succeed, for Benedict XIV testifies as to the large number shortly after the time of Pius V.[76] It is to their influence mainly that the congregations of today owe their origin. Thus there was a twofold development of Tertiaries, those living in common apart from the world, and those living at home in the world.[77] Most likely the former were anxious to be Tertiaries because of the numerous indulgences and favors attached to the Third Order since many Tertiary communities are found with solemn vows and the cloister. The canon speaks only of religious Tertiaries and only those which are congregations since we know the Code does not speak of new orders.

Aggregation signifies an affiliation of a Tertiary congregation to the first order so that it may participate in the indulgences and other spiritual favors of the first and second orders, without however, sacrificing its autonomy and independence, or its character as a congregation.[78] Thus a spiritual tie results, and the abundant favors and privileges that for centuries have been heaped upon these first orders by the Holy See are communicated to the affiliated congregation. This would not imply a juridical change in the status of the Tertiary congregation, or that it has the privilege of exemption similar to that of the first order.[79] Neither is any jurisdiction over

[75] Bouix, *De Regul.*, I, 316; Reinmann, *The Third Order Secular of St. Francis*, p. 25.

[76] Benedict XIV, *Inst. Eccl.*, *Inst.* 29, n. 18.

[77] Bouix, *De Regul.*, I, 316.

[78] Espelage, *Aggregation of Tertiaries*, p. 5. By a decree of the Sacred Congregation of Indulgences, Aug. 28, 1903, it was decided that these Tertiaries participate in all the indulgences of the first and second orders and that the Churches of Tertiaries also enjoy the same indulgences as the first and third orders. *Cf. A. S. S.*, 36, 377. S. Cong. of E. E. & Reg., decree, *"Auctis admodum"* of Jan. 30, 1905—*A. S. S.*, 37, 685.

[79] Schaefer, *De Rel.*, n. 73.

the congregation conferred upon the order by this affiliation,[80] as it is an affiliation of honor and creates no dependence of the one upon the other. The aggregation of an entire moral person is seemingly something new, as formerly only individuals as such were affiliated.[81]

Only orders are competent to aggregate, and those only that have been given this privilege by law. These are the Franciscans, Dominicans, Carmelites, Servites, Augustinians, and probably the Benedictines.[82] No other orders have the power to affiliate validly.[83] Of these orders the Supreme Moderator alone can validly aggregate. The Holy See at times and in individual cases aggregates as it did in the case of the Ursulines,[84] but in the majority of instances aggregation is left to the General of the first order.

If a new institute is desirous of being affiliated to one of the established orders it is proper to ask the General of this order before approaching the Holy See, as then the institute could make note of the General's willingness. In this canon the Code speaks of new institutes, though the same norms apply for already established communities. Where there are several branches of the first order, the General of each branch can affiliate. The very nature of aggregation demands that it be done by the Supreme Moderator of the first order. The Supreme Moderator can exercise this power independent of the consent of the Ordinary of the place as the power to communicate these privileges is not contingent upon the bishop's consent for its validity, though for diocesan communities he should have the bishop's consent.

---

[80] Vermeersch-Creusen, *Epitome*, I, n. 551; Larraona. *Comm. pro Rel.*, V (1924), 85.

[81] Larraona, *Comm. pro Rel.*, V (1924), 88.

[82] Espelage, *Aggregation of Tertiaries*, p. 6; Augustine, *A Commentary on Canon Law*, III, 69. He admits the uncertainty of the power of the Benedictines to affiliate since they have no Supreme Moderator in the sense of the Code.

[83] Canon 703, §1 and § 2, seems to give added force to this conclusion.

[84] S. Cong. of Reg., Decree, *Superiossae societatis*, June 30, 1911—*A. A. S.*, III (1911), 091.

As said before, if the bishop does not consult the Holy See before the foundation of the institute the aggregation would nevertheless stand. Any defect in aggregation would not, as is evident, affect the validity of the foundation of the religious congregation simply because the two are not intimately connected.[85] The validity of the aggregation is dependent upon the valid foundation but not *vice versa.* Nor does it seem, once the institute has been approved by the Holy See, that it is necessary to consult the Holy See in order to be aggregated, unless because of the aggregation a change should be demanded in anything that the Holy See has already approved.[86] For pontifical institutes this may at times be necessary, since oftentimes changes of greater or lesser import in the constitutions are necessary and no other power except the Holy See has a right to make these changes. As to delegation, since these Supreme Moderators possess this faculty by ordinary power they can and may delegate this to others.[87]

Certain conditions are placed on this canonical affiliation, which conditions, though not essential, yet are ordinarily required. The Tertiary congregation must have some similarity to the institute to which it is joined. Thus if a Tertiary congregation desires to be united to the Franciscans, its constitutions should be based, at least substantially, on the rule of the third order of St. Francis, or it must show its relationship to the Franciscan Order by its name and habit.[88] There should be some external bond or tie indicative of the spiritual relationship but this demand is not so rigid that exceptions will not be tolerated.[89]

---

[85] Toso, *Commentaria Minora,* lib. II, pars II, p. 15.

[86] Vermeersch-Creusen, *Epitome,* I, n. 551.

[87] Schaefer, *De Rel.,* n. 73.

[88] Espelage, *Aggregation of Tertiaries,* p. 7. Cf. also *Normae* (1901), n. 16.

[89] Thus a part of the garb of the first order should be worn or some other sign used to show aggregation. The scapular for good reasons is permitted to be worn, or if there are good reasons no insignia will be required by the Holy See. Cf. *Comm. pro Rel.,* V (1924), 84, footnotes 80 and 81; *A. S. S.,* 36, 606.

Practically the aggregation should be made in writing, though the law is silent on this point. Reason itself suggests this as the only feasable manner for it will then stand as a proof for future contingencies and remove any uncertainties which may arise. The documents should have the points which were mentioned above and be signed by the Supreme Moderator of the first order.

Article II.

Text. Can. 492, § 3. *Nec nomen nec habitus religionis iam constitutae assumi potest ab iis qui ad illam legitime non pertinent aut a nova religione.*

1. *Nomen.* This is added as a protection to the religious institutes already in existence which have made themselves known and which have done much to deserve esteem and honor. For through the name many connotations arise, and rightly it is held in honor by all the members and considered inalienable, as the sole possession of the first one entitled thereto. The law is purely equitable, but the reason of it evidently seems to be to avoid the confusion that otherwise might arise. A name is a characteristic mark whereby one person or one certain group may be distinguished from another but its uselessness would be apparent were several to take the same title.

As seen from history, the majority of the early religious institutes derived their titles from their founders, that is, the communities were called after them. A cursory glance shows such was generally the case, for we have the monks of Sts. Basil, Pachomius, Benedict, Columban, etc. Later, communities were designated by a name suggestive of the place of their origin, such are the Carthusians, Cistercians, and Carmelites. At the time of the rise of the mendicant orders the name was often suggestive of some outstanding trait, as the Order of Friars Minor, the Order of Preachers. With the growth of modern congregations, however, a diversification of customs arose, but the majority of the names of the last three centuries are indicative of the secondary scope of the institute thereby suggesting the main purpose of their establishment. Many too are called or named according to some attribute of God or His saints or after some phase of Christian veneration.

The Code merely gives a negative command to the end that no congregation should usurp the name of another community. It is supplemented by the *Normae* which are more explicit and positive and which state in general what names are becoming to religious institutes. It must be first understood before investigation of the law in what various senses and ways a name may be applied to a religious community. First, there is the official name, which it that title juridically recognized as actually belonging to the institute. Secondly, there is the common or popular name, that name which is most frequently used in ordinary conversation and by which sometimes an institute is commonly known. And thirdly, there is the abbreviated title of an institute. In the sense of the Code, strictly speaking, the word *title* or *name* applies only to the official name. However, usage often gives a community a name distinct from the official title yet very distinctive of that community, as the Jesuits, Claręntians. Those names too may be considered as proper, and any usurpation of such names would be reproved by the Holy See. The same may be said of an abbreviated title. A new society should see that its abbreviated name does not come in conflict with some other community's. Oftentimes the Holy See uses these abbreviations, and thus it seems to give its quasi-approbation to them. In practice the best mode of procedure should be, (a) in public acts and documents, that the religious family use its own official title; (b) in other acts of less importance it may use its popular or abbreviated title.[21]

The *Normae* of 1921, repeating in this case almost verbatim the *Normae* of 1901, declare that the title or the name of the

[21] Pejska, *Jus Can. Rel.*, p. 12.

religious congregation may be taken either from the attributes of God, or from the mysteries of our holy Religion, or from the feasts of our Lord and the Blessed Virgin, or from the saints, or from the special scope of the institute itself. From this it is evident that the Holy See does not look with favor upon the naming of future institutes after the founder, as the list does not include the names of founders as sources of titles.[92] Still the force of the law is not so great as to preclude absolutely every exception.

If an institute should take the name of another institute already in existence, something should be added to the title to make the distinction clear.[93] Thus in the United States there are any number of Franciscan communities distinguished by additional titles, such being, The Sisters of the Third Order of St. Francis, School Sisters of St. Francis, Franciscan Sisters of Christian Charity, etc.[94] A similar distinction prevails with regard to Dominican Sisterhoods.[95]

There is still another admonition to which attention must be given, and this caution refers to the propriety of a name. Care should be taken that the title of a religious congregation be neither too artificially constructed, nor that it express or insinuate any form of devotion not approved by the Holy See. The purpose of this is to retain a respect for the religious state which artificiality and excessive zeal do not bestow. A quality very much needed here is conciseness, tending both to brevity and clearness. It is but natural that the Holy See does not desire to give even an apparent approval to names implying beliefs which are not publicly approved by the Church or to names which oftentimes may be offensive to good taste.

At the time of consulting the Apostolic See before the foundation, the title of the community must be sent in also, and once the Holy See has approved this title it may not be changed

[92] N. 26—*A. A. S.*, XIII (1921), 318; *Normae* (1901), n. 39-41.
[93] Normae (1921), n. 27—*A. A. S.*, XIII (1921), 318.
[94] *The Official Catholic Year Book* (1928), p. 368 sq.
[95] *The Official Catholic Year Book* (1928), p. 366.

unless with the Holy See's consent. If there are good reasons this desired change will readily be granted. In the quinquennial report demanded of religious congregations by the Holy See, the Supreme Moderator must tell whether the name or the habit of the institute has at any time since its inception been changed, and if so, by what authority.[96]

The title should also be looked at from the standpoint of civil effects, inheritance, legacies and property. To avoid legal entanglements similarity of names should be avoided. It is clear that no private societies or any group in the world have the right to usurp the name of any established community, as they likewise are forbidden this by this canon.

II. *Habitus.* Historians can trace, from the earliest days of the Church the use of some special garb by those especially consecrated to Christ.[97] The reason for this change of garb upon entering a religious community is to signify a change of life. Two reasons militate in favor of a special garb or habit for religious: first, to show a proper profession, just as soldiers and sailors are attired in a special uniform; and the second, that the religious be known as such and thus always be obliged to live holily since all know him if he violates the laws of his profession.[98]

In general the desire of the Church is to see each institute have a special habit though she does not prescribe this by any general law. Some institutes have no special garb, as for example the Society of Jesus.[99] Many of the more recent congregations of men adopted the secular cassock with few modifications, which latter changes, if peculiar by cape, cincture, insignia, must be considered as the proper habit of that certain community.

[96] S. Cong. of Rel., Instruction, March 25, 1922, n. 3—A. A. S., XIV (1922), 278.

[97] Parsons, *Studies in Church History*, VI, 521 sq.; Augustine, *A Commentary on Canon Law*, III, 71.

[98] Bellarminus, L. II, *de Monach.*, cap. 40.

[99] Ojetti, *Synopsis Rer. Mor.*, n. 2277.

The respect for the habit of another community needed no special emphasis as long as the Benedictines were the only order, but when new communities arose this Papal provision had to be made.[100] For exteriorly it is precisely the habit that differentiates one institute from another. The Holy See is severe in enforcing this law of not infringing upon the habit of an already established community. Thus several centuries ago a decision of the Congregation of Bishops and Regulars was given in favor of the Dominicans who justly complained that another group was using a habit so similar to theirs that mistakes in identification could easily occur.[101] Hence once a habit is approved it is proper only to the institute for which it was approved, and this institute alone has a right to its use. Nor can this habit be changed without the consent of Rome.[102] To possess the right to have its own habit an institute must be canonically erected. There is no question but that this canon also forbids persons in the world from wearing the particular garb of any institute no matter what the motive of a person may be. In the early ages this provision was enforced by civil law.[103]

The later *Normae* (1921) do not refer explicitly to the habit, but in the earlier Normae quite a number of suggestions were made.[104] The omission of this explicit reference does not denote a change of attitude on the part of the Holy See. Any deviation from the earlier restrictions will speedily meet with a request from the Holy See that they be changed, and an order will be given to observe the customs and style as found agreeable to the eyes of the Church. The form, color and material of the habit should cause respect, justify religious dignity, and be consistent with the poverty professed. No gold or silver

[100] Zawart, *The Capuchins*, p. 27.

[101] May 8, 1595—*Fontes*, n. 1538.

[102] Cf. Can. 495, § 2; *Normae* (1901), n. 70; S. Cong. of Bish. & Reg., Pragen seu Militaris Ordinis Crucigerorum, April 27, 1883—*A. S. S.*, 16, 292; Ord. Excal. S. S. Trin., Cong. Ep. & Reg., March 18, 1904—*A. S. S.*, 36, 606.

[103] *Nov.*, 123, c. 44; *Basilica*, IV, 1, 16.

[104] Normae (1901), n. 66-70.

ornaments should be permitted, except perchance a small silver cross or medal. Neither silk nor anything that would bring ridicule upon the religious state will be allowed.

A distinctive habit may be had for the two classes of members but these habits should not be such that the one differs radically from the other, leaving the impression of two distinct communities. In all religious communities it is advisable and in most it is customary to make a slight distinction between the habit of the professed and that of the novices. The constitutions should describe the form of the habit exactly. When writing to the Holy See and sending a description of the habit it is best to send a model, such as a doll dressed in the habit adopted so that an exact idea may be had of the proposed religious garb. In some communities it is customary to wear a ring, as a sign of the mythical union with Christ. This should be of silver.[105]

---

[105] Vicente, *Inst. Rec.*, n. 161.

CHAPTER V

The Various Stages in the Approbation of Religious Institutes

The great difference that exists between the episcopal and papal approbation is well known and, since the papal excels the episcopal in extent, being wider and greater in effects and giving assurance of an unerring guidance, it is not in the least surprising that from the start, a new religious congregation will have this in view, to obtain a favorable decision concerning itself from the Holy See. In its early stages a new community is still in an imperfect condition. Though entirely an autonomous society, yet it is subject to many restrictions on the part of the bishop. Besides formerly if it should chance to spread into other dioceses many thing militated against unity which is a prime requisite in order that the institute preserve its original nature and purpose. In this respect nowadays it is well protected by the Code.[1] The aim of the new society will be to have firmness and stability, to be enriched with all the privileges and favors of Mother Church, which aim will not be fully obtained unless it has received the seal of definite approbation from the Head of all Christendom.

Thus it is evident that there are various steps or stages of approval in the life of a new community. As it grows stronger various immunities from the power of the bishop will be given, and special privileges will be granted according to the degree of the solidity of its foundation and its spread into various localities. It can correctly be said that at almost all times

[1] Canon 495, § 2.

to a certain degree there has been a distinction in approbation. and seldom, if ever, did the Holy See give her full and final approbation to an institute in the period of its infancy. In the first eleven centuries those that she approved were usually well established and had flourished for years, having given every evidence of their firmness and value to the Church.

Even in the thirteenth century when she reserved solely to herself the right to establish new communities her first approbation to these might be considered more in the light of a particular commission to begin, and then usually after a number of years, according to the growth and stability of the community, she gave her solemn approbation. Thus when the Order of St. Francis was founded, Pope Innocent III gave him permission to start in the year 1210,[2] and though the Pope caused the rule to be recognized by the Fourth Lateran Council, yet it was not until 1223 that the rule was solemnly approved.[3] Other examples of the same phenomenon could easily be shown proper to that time and subsequent periods.[4] This was not however, a matter of the observance of any general law, but rather a question of prudence. For time alone can teach us concerning the practical value of new institutes, and so they were first permitted to exist and only after a suitable time did the Holy See give a solemn and definite approbation to them.

As now established the distinction in the manner of approbation is but of recent origin. Indirectly its origin is traced

---

[2] Cuthbert, *Life of St. Francis of Assisi*, p. 102.

[3] Const., *"Solet annuere,"* November 29, 1223—Constitutiones Ord. Min. Conventualium S. Francisci, p. 4.

[4] A good example of later centuries is that of the Passionists founded by St. Paul of the Cross. Though the stages of approval were not strictly juridical nor definitely determined at this time, yet the manner in which the Holy See acted shows how she oftentimes proceeded in similar cases. In 1735 the Passionists received the oral approval of Benedict XIII, and permission to assemble associates; on May 15, 1741, Benedict XIV gave them the formal approval of the rule; on November 16, 1769, Clement XIV raised the institute to the dignity of a canonical congregation with all the rights and privileges of other orders; and finally on September 15, 1775, they were solemnly approved by Pius VI. Cf. Purcell, "*The* Bicentenary of the Passionists," *Cath. World*, 112 (1920), 513.

back to the famous Constitution "*Quamvis iusto*" of Benedict XIV, in paragraph 13 of which he states the congregation in question was entirely subject to the local Ordinary.[5] But only in the nineteenth century did the distinction in the stages of approval become clear and well defined through the style and unchanging practice of the Congregation of Bishops and Regulars. From that time on any number of examples can be brought to show that the stages of approbation were similar to the practice that prevails today.[6] This latter is a continuation of the earlier practice brought on by custom and juridically sanctioned for the first time by Leo XIII, who made a clear distinction between diocesan and pontifical institutes.[7] Before this time the Holy See would not approve an institute unless it had been diocesan for some time, and at the most in the earlier stages would praise the scope and spirit of the founder.[8]

This division is now sanctioned by the new Code and thus the chief division of religious institutes, as far as their canonical status is concerned, is that of diocesan and pontifical. A *religio iuris pontificii*, as the Code calls it, is every institute

[5] April 30, 1749—*Fontes*, n. 398.

[6] Bizzarri, p. 808 sq.; Vicente, *Inst. Rec.*, pp. 18-27.

[7] Const., "*Conditae a Christo*," December 8, 1900—Fontes, n. 644.

[8] Bizzarri, *op. cit.*, 772. In this place Bizzarri states clearly the method by which an institute could receive approbation from the Holy See in the nineteenth century, the conditions and also the customary stages. When asking for approbation of any institute, letters of commendation must be obtained from each bishop of the various places where the institute has a house or houses. The request should then be sent through the bishop of the diocese where the first foundation was, or where the principal house was, and this request should mention the scope, foundation, number of houses, brethren or sisters, means of sustenance, utility, progress, etc., of the community. If the institute was but recently erected, and had but one or two houses and no complete constitutions then the scope or purpose of the founder was praised. After a seasonable time, when the institute had spread to various localities and bore great fruit, and had received the commendation of the Ordinary, then it received the decree of praise (*decretum laudis*), and sometimes even of approbation, especially if the constitutions were satisfactory. The constitutions were not approved unless they had been tried for some time and had been changed according to suggestions from the Holy See. Generally a temporary approbation of the constitutions preceded (three or five years), and then the decree of definite approbation followed. Cf. Bizzarri, *Collectanea*, 772.

which has obtained from the Apostolic See either approbation or at least the decree of commendation (*decretum laudis*); while a diocesan institute is one erected by the Ordinary and which has not yet obtained this decree of commendation.[9] This division is of the greatest importance in canon law as so many effects and rights are dependent on these respective states. To know these rights it is equally important to understand the status of the institute and to which of these two categories it belongs.

But since we are concerned here, not so much with the rights of the congregations, but their approval as the source of these rights, a somewhat different method of considering them is followed. Many methods are possible but the best plan seems to be that which considers the stages of approval as four distinct steps, one step succeeding closely upon the other. These four are: first, the canonical establishment through the approval of the bishop; second, the decree of commendation by the Holy See; third, the definite approbation of the institute with the simultaneous temporary approval of the constitutions; and fourth, the final and definite approbation of the constitutions. Thus there is but one stage to the episcopal approbation and ordinarily three to the papal. It need hardly be stated that such is the ordinary mode in which this occurs, but there are many occasions for exceptions. Oftentimes for sufficient reasons the approbation of the institute may be given immediately without a decree of commendation preceding, and so too with the constitutions, as they may be approved finally and definitely, simultaneously with the approbation of the institute. But exceptions such as these do not change the usual practice which holds in the majority of cases and is given as a regular method in the two *Normae* published in 1901 and 1921, which form a sort of code or guide in affairs relating to the establishment of religious congregations. Exceptions to these rules may be said to be extraordinary ways of receiving approbation.[10]

[9] Canon 488, 3°.
[10] Aquilar, *Scientia Jur.*, p. 271.

Article 1

Diocesan Institutes

Canon 492, § 2. *Congregatio juris dioecesani, quamvis decursu temporis in plures dioceses diffusa, usque tamen dum pontificiae approbationis aut laudis testimonio caruerit, remanet dioecesana, Ordinariorum jurisdictioni ad norman juris plane subjecta.*

It was the act and will of the bishop that gave the new congregation its existence and, since a creation of his is subject entirely to his authority it is rightly called diocesan, as that is the extent of his jurisdiction, though in due time the institute may later spread to various dioceses. This extent can only be through the willingness of the various bishops, and the consent of several can not change the institute from a diocesan to a pontifical. Neither did the permission of the Holy See for erection make it a pontifical institute, unless the decree explicitly stated so. In the beginning the Apostolic See does not give approbation when granting permission to the bishop to make the foundation. It considers the principal facts relative to the proposed congregation and being satisfied nothing harmful is proposed, by the letter of permission disclaims any objection to the plan porposed, leaving it to the bishop to make the foundation. If the Pope were to approve directly and on his own initiative then the institute would immediately become a pontifical community.[12]

There is no question but that the bishop confers true personality. The diocesan institute thus has the real nature of a religious society with all the rights that belong any objection to the plan proposed, leaving it to the bishop to diocesan religious can not be called corporations in the ecclesiastical sense, as they lack autonomy or independence.[14] The

[12] Larraona, *Comm. pro Rel.*, V (1924), 42.

[13] S. Cong. de Rel., Decretum, "*Quod iam,*" November 30, 1922—A. A. S., XIV (1922), 644.

[14] Augustine, *A Commentary on Canon Law,* III, 70.

Ordinary has it is true very extensive power over these, but it is of that kind which does not destroy the college of persons. Hence it is rightfully said that his power is as extensive as the moral person will permit to be suffered without itself being destroyed.[15] Granted that the bishop is in charge of the diocesan institute he has no jurisdiction in the internal affairs.[16] Often the Congregation of Religious has insisted on this that no bishop be elected and allowed to be the superior of the institute with dominative power.[17]

The religious superior alone has the dominative power over his subjects,[18] which is similar to the father's in a family and which arises not from the keys or power of the Church, but rather through the will of those professing a certain constitution and promising obedience to it.[19] With all this amplitude of power whereby the new congregation is entirely subject to the jurisdiction of the Ordinary according to the law,[20] it is exceedingly difficult to place exact limits on its exercise. Some even go so far as to give him authority in internal affairs, which seems hardly tenable. He can not be said to be *de gremio*, nor even the head of the chapter though he may preside according to the Code.[21] Sometimes when one comes to a particular point it is very difficult to express and define how far his power extends. He can not trepass upon the internal affairs of a community[22] but the difficulty at times is to determine what is an internal affair. In many matters of internal government the bishop has mere supervision and not the decision. Even as religious they acknowledge the bishop as superior and must

---

[15] Toso, *Commentaria Minora*, Lib. II, Pars II, p. 49.

[16] Lanslots, *A Handbook of Canon Law*, p. 12.

[17] Bizzarri, *Animadversiones*, p. 778, III, 1; 779, IV, 1; 779, V, 1; 788, XIII, 1; 789, XIV, 2. These are all cases of diocesan institutes seeking pontifical approbation.

[18] Vromant, *Jus Miss.*, n. 47, ad 3.

[19] Suarez, *De Rel.*, III, L. II, c. 18, n. 5.

[20] Canon 492, § 2.

[21] Cf. S. Cong. Concilii, *Dioecesis V.*, March 13, 1921—*A. A. S.*, XIII (1921), 440.

[22] Zitelli, *Apparatus Jur. Eccl.*, p. 24; Schaefer, *De Rel.*, n. 71.

obey as the other faithful do and so the vow is also made to the bishop.[23] In many respects the Code has been more gracious to these diocesan communities than any previous laws.

The main objective of a diocesan congregation should be so to labor that it will reach such a stage of development in which it will be worthy to receive the decree of praise from Rome, for until it receives this something always will seem to be lacking to it.[24] *Per se* they are not even exempt from the jurisdiction of the pastor of the place, though the bishop can grant exemption from the local parish and if conditions warrant, it would be expedient for the bishop to grant exemption.[25]

The early years of a new community are experimental, at least in a way, but of all the trying circumstances which must be faced that of forming the constitutions is the hardest. No law prescribes that it be written before the foundation of the new congregation, though it is better that this be done; nor is it required that the constitutions be sent to Rome for inspection when permission is asked to start. Generally history tells us that rules for most orders were written after their foundation and when they were actually functioning. They were the fruit of much deliberation on the part of both founder and associates. As finally written they were the result of many hours of prayer, of many months of experience and often of the aid of wiser men.[26] Or else they were the adaptations of some previous rule the value of which was shown by experience, so modified as to suit the individual requirements and the peculiar scope of the congregation. But nowadays with the present development of constitutions according to the Code and the *Normae* of 1901 there is little reason for much delay.

The earliest monks had no written rule. The example of the leader was the rule, his word alone was the law.[27] But such could not last long and soon after we find the first rule of St.

[23] Vermeersch-Creusen, *Epitome,* I, n. 568.

[24] Bizzarri, *Collectanea,* p. 145.

[25] Canon 464, § 2; Augustine, *Rights and Duties of Ordinaries,* p. 76.

[26] Purcell. "The Bicentenary of the Passionist Order"—*Cath. World,* 112 (1920-1921), 517.

[27] Heimbucher, *Die Orden und Kong.,* I, 33.

Pachomius,[28] which was followed later by St. Benedict's, St. Basil's, St. Columban's, St. Augustine's, and St. Francis'. In the middle ages the four recognized by the Church officially were the rules of Sts. Basil, Benedict, Augustine, and Francis.[29] These are called the great rules because they have served as the foundation for many others and have been decorated with special praises.[30] Through the influence of the Fourth Lateran Council prohibiting new rules and demanding that new Orders take some approved rule,[31] no new rules were established for several centuries. This was followed so strictly that in those days a community was not considered a religious society unless it followed some approved rule.[32] With the growth of the congregations new constitutions also came in force and because of the enforcement of the laws against the use of the word "rule"[33] and also in order to distinguish them from the four rules the newer communities have called their laws *constitutions*.

Some rule, or constitution, or whatever name it may be, is required not necessarily by divine law but by ecclesiastical law.[34] The Church could permit the personal direction of the superior to be the rule or constitution, but in many cases this produces only disorder as it subjects the members to the vagaries and fancies of another. A certain rule is found necessary by experience, otherwise not order but confusion results, and such life could not be called the school of perfection.[35] And the gravest concern should be shown in framing a good constitution for upon this more than all things else does the future of the new community hinge.

---

[28] Raus, *De Sac. Obedientiae Voto,* n. 78, p. 148.
[29] Wernz, *Jus Dec.,* III, n. 596.
[30] Schaefer, *De Rel.,* n. 51, 3.
[31] Mansi, XXII, 1002.
[32] Bouix, *De Reg.,* I, 197; In Clem, *De Rel. Domibus,* IX, 3.
[33] Normae (1901), n. 32.
[34] Wernz, *Jus Dec.,* III, n. 591; Vicente, *Inst. Rec.* n. 27, p. 13; Larraona, Commentarium Codicis,—*Comm. pro Rel.,* II, 207.
[35] Suarez, *De Rel.,* III, L. II, c. 17, n. 14.

A rule or constitution is a norm of life, by which the subjects in a community are directed towards God. By it the subject is regulated in a fourfold manner in his relation to God, the world, himself, and his brethren.[36] It is a plan of life imposed on the members to help them work in common on the basis of the spirit of the Gospel.[37] Practically a twofold end should be in mind when forming these constitutions. They should fix and determine the various duties which the members are to accept, the extent of the vows, the exercises of piety and charity, and also to determine the rights that flow to all; and secondly, they should ordain all that pertains to government so that confusion be avoided and arbitrariness guarded against.[38] As it should provide against all evils that ordinarily occur it must be complete in every detail. Besides it must be in conformity with the laws of the Church, for since older communities are obliged to change theirs according to the new Code[39] the Holy See will be much more insistent that newer ones observe the new law. The inability of a person unaided and not well versed in canon law to conform his constitutions to those of the Code is apparent, and nowadays this should be done under the guidance of an expert well versed in law, whom the bishop should appoint, not as the author but as a helper to the founder. In all cases the bishop is the final arbiter in diocesan congregations though he must always keep in mind the *Normae* of 1901 and 1921. He alone promulgates and makes the constitutions particular laws. Due time should be taken in their formation and thereby assurance be had of good results.[39b]

A distinction is made only in older orders between the rule and constitution. This arose partly because of the deficiency of these rules and partly as a consequence to the decree of

---

[36] St. Bonaventure, *Opera Omnia*, VIII, Opus, 17, n. 0, (p. 409).

[37] *The New Cath. Dictionary*, p. 889.

[38] Larraona, *Comm. pro Rel.*, II (1921), 207.

[39] S. Cong. of Rel., decree, *Ad normam Canonis*, June 26, 1918—*A. A. S.*, X (1918), 290.

[39b] Cf. Vermeersch, *De Conscribendis Const.*, *Periodica*, XVI, (1927), 41x—46x; 107x—114x; 154x—172x.

the Fourth Lateran Council whereby a new order adopting an old rule could still by particular interpretation of these obtain its special purpose. The difference between the constitution and rule where this distinction is now followed is this; the rules are more ancient and common to many religious orders, whereas the constitutions are interpretations of the rules and proper to each institute;[40] the rules are approved by the Roman Pontiff, but not always the constitutions;[41] finally, the rules are considered as perpetual and immutable because they are regarded as fundamental laws, whereas the constitutions may be changed and oftentimes are in order to make the regulations suitable and adaptable to the times. Four qualities shine thus preeminently in the rules: antiquity, authority, dignity, and firmness.[42]

The wish of the Church concerning the word to be used to designate the particular laws of a community is expressed in the *Normae*.[43] Therein it is demanded that any terms of canon law that can not be applied to religious congregations should be excluded from the constitutions, and as an example it explicitly mentions as forbidden the word "rule", in place of which the word "constitution" should be used. It has been the general practice of the Holy See not to permit the distinction between rule and constitution in new institutes of the past two centuries.[44] This holds for both new rules and constitutions adopted simultaneously, for if a new congregation wishes to base its constitution on some old rule all that is required is to see that it faithfully copy the rule and make no changes.[45] From experience it is apparent though that exceptions have been made, for the word "rule" has been

[40] Schaefer, *De Rel.*, n. 54; Bouix, *De Reg.*, II, P. VI, s. 5, c. 4, § 1.
[41] Schaefer, *op. cit.*, n. 54; Wernz, *Jus Dec.*, III, n. 596.
[42] Pejska, *Jus Can. Relig.*, p. 21.
[43] *Normae* (1921), n. 22, h—*A. A. S.*, XIII (1921), 317; *Normae* (1901), n. 32.
[44] Bizzarri, *op. cit.*, p. 782, VIII, 2; Larraona, *Comm. pro Rel.*, I (1920), 176.
[45] Vicente, *Inst. Rec.*, n. 120, p. 53.

used by new congregations not in the old sense but in the new.[46] But in the light of the new *Normae* the Holy See is apt to force a change if terms are used which do not conform to her laws. Nowadays the terms which are used to designate the sum total of regulations adopted by a new congregation are statues, constitutions, norms and ordinations. The first two terms are the more common.

The constitutions are therefore the special laws of a religious community. The style thereof should be simple, clear, and to the point.[47] All verbosity and uncanonical terms should be avoided. The terminology of canon law as contained in the Code should be adhered to wherever possible. Brevity will be a great help to the memory,[48] and perspicacity will truly be obtained through the use of words which have the sanction of centuries. If the law is to be a guide to sanctity, it should preclude all doubts whenever possible so that no dissensions may later arise as to the meaning. These notes are apparent viewing it solely from the logical standpoint. The Holy See also has special recommendations to make. It should always be remembered that these recommendations are not strictly laws, but rather are given as guides that when the institute approaches the Holy See later on, the negotiations may more swiftly and easily be completed.[49]

All prefaces, introductions, proems, historical notes, letters of exhortation or praise, except the decree of commendation or approbation which are later given, should be excluded.[50] Citations of scripture texts, of the Councils, of the Fathers, of theologians, or whatever books or authors, do not belong in the constitutions. Peculiar directories, ceremonials, or manuals, customs or uses of the congregation should not be included less they seem to be approved. No mention ought to be made of

[46] Larraona, *Comm. pro Rel.*, I (1920), 176, n. 30; Lanslots, *A Handbook of Canon Law*, p. 10.

[47] Bizzarri, *op. cit.*, 795, XVII, 20.

[48] Vicente, *Inst. Rec.*, n. 120, p. 53.

[49] *Normae* (1921), n. 2 b—*A. A. S.*, XIII (1921), 312.

[50] *Normae* (1921), n. 22.

civil laws for approbation. The constitutions should not prescribe the duties and offices of bishops or confessors as these laws are not made for them. An order of studies and the plan of the day should not be too minutely described. It should avoid all theological disputes and controverted doctrines in the matter of vows. Terms which do not pertain to religious congregations should not be used. Long drawn out ascetical instructions and spiritual exhortations which belong to ascetical books have no place in a law book which ought to contain constitutional laws directing the acts of the community either as regards the government or as regards discipline and the spiritual life. Minute descriptions relative to the secondary offices are unbecoming. Finally any disposition which is implicitly or explicitly against the general law must be excluded. These admonitions are based upon the experiences of the last century and contain those things which the Church has often found necessary to expunge as unfit or unbecoming in one way or another.[51]

In general the constitutions should contain all that pertains to the nature, vows, members, and the manner of living of the religious congregation; also the form of government, the administration, and the officers.[52] All these can be divided into two, three, or four parts but above all briefness, clearness and good order are commendable. To make it easy for reference the constitution should be divided into parts, the parts into chapters, the chapters into articles or paragraphs. Each section should be numbered and the numbers should be consecutive from the beginning to the end.[53]

Apparently the time when the constitutions are first formed is the best and most suitable time for following these suggestions, as it will necessarily be done if the institute wishes to expand under Rome's approval. So in the formation of these constitutions the *Normae* of 1921 as also the second part of

[51] Cf. Bizzarri, *op. cit.*, pp. 773-807, who enumerates the corrections made in twenty-one constitutions of different congregations from 1858-1861.

[52] *Normae* (1921), n. 23—*A. A. S.*, XIII (1921), 318.

[53] *Normae* (1921), n. 24-25.

the *Normae* of 1901, and the Code should be followed scrupulously as otherwise deviations from these standards may cause a long delay in later papal approval. But circumstances of time and place will often be sufficient reasons for minor deviations from these regulations.

The bishop approves the constitutions of diocesan communities. He is also free to change them with due regard, however, to the *jus quaesitum,* and provided he does not infringe on any of those points that had the Holy See's approval.[54] The reason is simple, since he alone creates the congregation and gives the rules their power he alone is the proper authority to make changes. Difficulties occurred former whenever a diocesan institute later spread out over several dioceses and each bishop was competent to change, with ill effects to the unity of the congregation as can well be seen.[55] The *Conditae* of Leo XIII changed this and demanded that no changes be made without the consent of all the Ordinaries,[56] which demand is repeated in the Code also.[57] This consent of the Ordinaries must be unanimous, and not only by majority vote, for what touches all as individuals must be approved by all.[58] This would not, however, prevent their coming to some agreement and permitting one of their number to have full authority for all changes.[59]

Sometimes letters are sent by the Holy See to the founder of an institute, praising his good intentions or the scope of the foundation.[60] These are given when an institute is quite

[54] Vermeersch-Creusen, *Epitome,* I, n. 554; Laurentius, *Inst. Jur. Eccl.,* n. 780, p. 581; Schaefer, *op. cit.,* n. 76.

[55] Some particular Councils suggested going to the Apostolic See if the bishops couldn't agree, or advised the religious congregation to seek the approbation of the Holy See once it had spread into various dioceses. Cf. Decreta Conc. Prov. Remensis (1853)—*Coll. Lac.,* IV, 171 c; Acta et Decreta Conc. Plen. Amer. Latinae (1899), n. 324.

[56] *Conditae a Christo,* § 1, n. 5—Fontes, n. 644.

[57] Canon 495, § 2.

[58] Canon 101, § 1, 2°; Vermeersch-Creusen, *Epitome,* I, n. 554, Reg. 29, R. J. in VI°.

[59] Larraona, *Comm. pro Rel.,* V (1924), 262-263.

[60] Normae (1901), n. 1.

new and has only one or the other house and the constitutions are not fully and completely tested. Either the Ordinary or the founder commended by him, makes known the character of the institute to the Supreme Pontiff and the good expected of it, to the end that it obtain the Apostolic Benediction. This blessing and praise in no way changes the institute and by this action the Holy See sees fit to extol the virtues of the congregation without however approving it and the institute still remains diocesan. The new *Normae* are silent regarding this praise of the scope but there seems to be no inclination to discontinue this practice.

Article II

Pontifical Institutions

§ I. Decretem Laudis.

Canon 488—*In canonibus qui sequuntur, venient nomine*: . . . . 3°. *Religionis juris pontificii, religio quae vel approbationem vel saltem laudis decretum ab Apostolica Sede est consecuta.*

An institute remains diocesan until it has received at least this decree of commendation (decretum laudis), which when obtained changes the institute into a pontifical institute with all the rights that such is entitled to by the Code.[61] The decree of commendation is the second stage of life through which a community ordinarily passes. It does not indicate approval in the full sense, yet it is a sign that the institute is pleasing to the Holy See and is worthy of praise because of the high ideals it holds and the good work it accomplishes. It affects the institute as such, not merely the scope, purpose or work and so differs from the mere praise of the good intentions of the founder as also from the permission granted to the bishop to found. The effects of this decree of commendation are

[61] Normae (1921), n. 6.

greater blessings on the community, the strengthening of unity, the conferring of many privileges and the withdrawal of much power previously held by the bishop over the community. The rights of the bishop must be judged from the Code,[62] unless some special privileges or very unusual exemptions should be granted by the decree.

The question arises as to the opportune time to seek this decree of praise from the Holy See. It is considered proper to ask for this when ten or fifteen years have elapsed since the foundation, but this is not so firmly set that there is no room for exception if other considerations are favorable.[63] But the time is of less importance than the growth and expansion of the institute. Also it should have shown the fruits of piety and have been observant of the vows of religion.[64] A notable number of members should be in a community and several houses established. The spread to other dioceses is considered the best reason for asking the approbation of the Holy See,[65] because in that case there would be as many heads as there are bishops of the places were the community is established and this multiplied government is not conducive to unity.[66] Even if the institute has not spread to other dioceses but has shown other signs of growth, it may rightly seek the Holy See's approval though it is not customary on the part of the Holy See to grant this under these circumstances.[67] A community which intends to remain in one diocese is not readily granted approval by the Holy See.[68]

The method and way to obtain this decree of commendation is clearly defined by the *Normae.*[69] First, a letter signed by the Supreme Moderator and his assistants or counsellors must be sent to the Supreme Pontiff asking for the decree

---

[62] *Normae* (1921), n. 6.
[63] *Normae* (1901), n. 9; Vicente, *Inst. Rec.* n. 100, p. 46.
[64] Normae (1921), n. 7.
[65] Laurentius, *Inst. Jur. Eccl.*, p. 580.
[66] Const., "Conditae a Christo," *Fontes*, 644.
[67] Wernz, *Jus Decr.*, III, n. 610.
[68] Zitelli, *Apparatus Jur. Ecc.*, p. 240.
[69] *Normae* (1921), n. 8.

of praise. This letter of course is sent to the Congregation of Religious or to the Congregation of the Propaganda or the Congregation of the Orientals according as one or the other has jurisdiction in the case. Practically in all cases in our regions the Congregation of Religious will have jurisdiction. The counsellors referred to here are those mentioned in canon 516, § 1. No mention is made of a community vote as it seems so apparent that this petition will be agreeable to all. Thinking that no objections wil be made, the Holy See presumes that all concur in this action.

Secondly, the letter from the community is not only to give an account of the origin and foundation of the community and the name of its founder, but also to include the principal qualities of the congregation. Likewise it should tell in detail the personal, disciplinary, material and economic state of the community; and give additional information regarding the institution of the novitiate, the number and the training of novices and postulants. The bishop of the principal house must testify to the authenticity and the truth of the document. The principal house does not necessarily mean the first one but rather the one where the highest Superior and the Council habitually reside. This attestation of the bishop should be on the same document which the officers of the community sign in order to avoid all mistakes.

Thirdly, testimonial letters are required from each and every Ordinary in whose diocese the community has a house or houses.[70] The episcopal seal should be affixed to each letter and then each must be sent secretly to the Holy See. The reason for secrecy is that the bishop may speak his mind freely which could not be done if he forwarded his letter through the community.[71] So his letter must not be sent through the Superior of the congregation but directly to the Holy See.[72] In this way he may inform the Congregation of Religious regarding anything he

[70] *Normae* (1921), n. 7.

[71] S. Cong. Ep. et Reg., circular letter, "*Usuvenit,*" June 22, 1900—*A. S. S.*, 33, 415.

[72] Vermeersch, *De Rel.*, II, p. 133.

deems necessary to say about this congregation. In the letter his opinion should be given about the institute, its work and methods. He should state whether it is an opportune time for approbation or whether the commendation of the Holy See should be deferred, and finally indicate the changes advisable in the institution itself or in its constitutions.[73]

Fourthly, the constitutions, acknowledged and approved by the bishop, and with the changes to meet the requested change of status, must also be sent by the community. These must usually be written in Latin, Italian, or French, and ought to be printed. This does not exclude the possibility of having the rules drawn up in the vernacular, but if this latter is different from one of the above three mentioned languages it must be translated into one of those tongues. In that case there does not seem to be any reason why it need be printed, and typewritten copies seem to suffice. The most convenient way is to have two parallel columns on the same page, the vernacular in one column, Latin, French, or Italian in the other, so that the work may be expedited. The pages, however, should be bound together firmly. A letter of the Sacred Congregation of Religious of March 24, 1914, requests that at least ten copies be sent.[74] The reason is to give all the men in the special commission appointed to examine the constitutions a chance to inspect these at their convenience.

It will be seen that the examination of the constitutions and their approval is considered a matter of the greatest moment, and because it demands so much labor a special commission was created just for this purpose on the authority of Pius X to examine the constitutions of new congregations. Besides, the Pope made it obligatory that all matters of this sort be referred to this commission which is a part of the Congregation of Religious.[75] If the consultors composing this

[73] Vicente, *Inst. Rec.*, n. 109, p. 49.

[74] Decree, "Peculiari curae," March 24, 1914, *Normae Peculiares*, II, n. 1—*A. A. S.*, VI (1914), 190.

[75] Sac. Cong. of Rel., decree, "*Peculiari curae*," March 24, 1914—*A. A. S.* VI (1914), 189.

commission can not come to any agreement then only should the matter be taken before the whole body of the Congregation of Religious. The special commission itself consists of the Cardinal Prefect and various consultors, one of whom is appointed secretary. The number of the consultors has varied from year to year as can be seen from looking over its lists, though now the full commission consists of 12 consultors.[76]

When a petition then is sent to the Congregation of Religious for approbation or commendation the Cardinal Prefect appoints one of the consultors of this special body to make the examination and gives him all the documents in the case. His duty is to investigate thoroughly and afterwards give his opinion in writing. Then his opinion, printed, is distributed to each one of the members, together with a copy of the constitution, at least ten days before they have their meeting. If they think it necessary or useful they may call in the interested party so that they may be enabled to understand all things more fully. On the day appointed for the meeting all should be present under the presidency of the Cardinal Prefect. At this meeting they will vote on the proposition whether and in what manner the petition of the religious congregation should be satisfied. Nothing is said about unanimous consent, but it is stated that if grave differences arise it is left to the judgment of the Prefect to reserve judgment in the matter to the Cardinals who form the Sacred Congregation of Religious. Finally the resolution signed by the Cardinal Prefect must be subjected by him to His Holiness for approbation,[77] and then only will he take care that the decree is put into effect.

[76] Thus in 1917 there were seven men on the commission. Cf. *Annuario Pontificio* (1917), p. 342. In 1921, probably because of the large number of institutes desirous of having their constitutions revised according to the Code, there were twelve men on the commission. Cf. *Annuario Pontificio* (1921), p. 389.

[77] *"Normae Peculiares,"* March 24, 1914, n. 11.—*A. A. S.*, VI (1914), 191. This was already demanded in 1854. Cf. Lucidi, *De Visitatione*, II, p. 133, n. 12; Colomiatti, *Codex Jur. Pontif.* II, p. 157: "In hujusmodi vero negotiis expediendis omnia debent referri Summo Pontifici; quin immo S. Smus. D. N. Pius P. P. IX, in audientia habita (22 sep. 1854), mandavit, ut in posterum supplicationes pro laudatione vel approbatione

The expenses of all this are to be borne by the community interested, and it is obliged to deposit a certain sum of money to defray all expenses, which sum will be determined by the prudent judgment of the secretary in each particular case.[78]

It is especially useful to ask here whether it is required to send in the various books that the institute may have, such as contain the customs and usages of the community, or the books that have the proper prayers which are recited in common. By a special decree of March 29, 1919, this was demanded of all religious congregations approved by the Holy See and in it it was stated that "the same be demanded in approving new institutes."[79] The wording of the decree seems to demand this only when the institute is approved, but approval here is used in its widest sense to include also the commendation of Rome and so by reason of this decree these books must also be sent at this time for the inspection of the commission.[80]

The action of the commission in examining the constitutions at this time does not in any manner indicate a direct approval of them. The decree of commendation has reference principally to the institute indicating a distinction between the constitutions and the institute itself. As conditions are today the decree by which the constitutions are approved is considered more solemn and of greater moment than the approval of the institute. Certainly the former is harder to obtain and is generally last in the order of time.[81] Its proper purpose in examining now is to make corrections where they are deemed necessary. For with the decree of commendation of the institute are generally given suggestions or observations regarding the constitutions and corrections and changes are made by the Sacred Congregation. The time is then fixed, say a period of five, seven, or ten years, when they must again be shown to

---

alicujus Instituti et constitutionum confirmatione, antequam quidquam a S. Congregatione agatur, Summo Pontifici referantur."

[78] *Normae Peculiares*, II, n. 6—A. A. S., VI (1914), 190.

[79] S. Cong. of Rel., Decree, "*In Congregatione Generali*," May 22, 1919—*A. A. S.*, XI (1919), 239.

[80] Schaefer, *De Rel.*, n. 55; Fanfani, *De Jure Rel.*, n. 10, 2° b.

[81] Vicente, *Inst. Rec.*, n. 99, p. 45.

the Sacred Congregation in their amended form.[82] If too many corrections are needed some little delay would result before everything was corrected, amended, added or subtracted as demanded. The Congregation of Religious has many times delayed action in the past because of some prominent defects,[83] though it would not do this if anything objectionable were found in the books containing the customs or the private prayers.

Fifthly, if any Tertiary community applies for this decree of commendation, it must have besides all the above requirements the testimony of the General Moderator of the first order to prove that it was canonically affiliated to the same first order according to canon 492, § 1.

After all things have been taken care of according to the wish of the Sacred Congregation of Religious the decree of commendation (*decretum laudis*) is then given. The form of the decree may differ as to wording in each case but the matter is invariably the same. It mentions briefly the history of the founding of the new congregation, its title, scope, vows, the form of government and concludes thus: 'SSmus Dominus Noster N . . . . , attentis litteris commendatitiis Antistitum, quorum in diocesibus Instituti, de quo agitur, domus reperiuntur, Institutum ipsum, uti Congregationem religiosam sub regimine Moderatoris Generalis . . . , praesentis Decreti tenore, amplissimis verbis laudat ac commendat; salva Ordinariorum jurisdictione ad norman sacrorum canonum." [84]

The effect of this is that the institute is now a pontifical institute. Since the action of the Holy See does not consist in any approbation it may be viewed in the light of an encouragement. For the Holy See has viewed the past efforts and has placed the institute under her guidance as an incentive to still greater labors, as an encouragement to continue to strive for and live in their noble purpose. The religious institute re-

[82] *Normae* (1912), n. 21 a—*A. A. S.,* XIII (1921), 316.
[83] Cf. Bizzarri, *op. cit.,* pp. 143, 145.
[84] Normae (1921), n. 6.

ceives all the rights of a pontifical congregation, chief among which is a partial exemption from the power of the bishop whose power suffers a great diminution after this decree.[85] Its laws or constitutions may no longer be changed except by the Holy See, this being clear from the law itself[86] and also from the nature of the case.[87]

II. *The Decree of Approbation of the Institute and the Approbation of the Constitutions by Way of Experiment.* From the title of this section it will be seen that two distinct objects are considered, namely the institute itself and its constitutions. The reason for this is evident since ordinarily both come together, that is, usually when the institute as such is approved there is generally added a decree of approbation of the constitutions by way of experiment for some defined time.[88]

When the congregation or community has received the decree of praise it should wait some time before approaching Rome seeking the approbation of the institute. The length of time is not definitely mentioned, but logically it must be sufficient time to test out the various changes that have been ordered by the Holy See and also to allow the community to grow in numbers. Irrespective of other considerations a period of five to ten years would seem ample and agreeable to Rome, since five or seven years are usually specified as the time to wait between the temporary approval of the constitutions and their definite approval.[89]

To obtain this decree of approbation of the institute and at the same time the temporary approval of the constitutions the *Normae* prescribed that the institute must demonstrate that it is a stable and well-knit society not broken by dissensions,

[85] Piat, *Prael. Jur. Reg.*, II, q. 126; Pejska, *Jus Can. Rel.*, p. 19.

[86] *Normae* (1921), n. 21 a; Vermeersch-Creusen, *Epitome*, I, 554.

[87] Benedict XIV, *De Synod. Dioec.*, T. I, L. IX, c. 1, n. 6.

[88] *Normae* (1921), n. 21 b.

[89] Cf. Approbationes de S. Cong. de Religiosis—A. A. S., XIV (1922), 164, 354; Approbationes de S. Cong. de Religiosis—A. A. S., XV (1923), 29, etc.

that the members are habitually observing the constitutions, that nothing objectionable has occurred in the administration of temporal affairs, but rather that all things have been rightly conducted. The zeal of the religious to observe the discipline and to cultivate charity towards one another must be rightly shown and also a zealous fulfilling of the proper work towards others.[80]

All these must be made known to the Apostolic See when asking for approbation at this stage. Petition for this decree must be done through the letter of the Supreme Moderator, authenticated by the bishop of the principal house, as was done previously. Furthermore each bishop in whose diocese the community has a house must also send a letter to Rome under the same conditions as required when the decree of commendation was sought. Thus the same kind of documents and the same methods that were essential before the decree of commendation was obtained are considered as essential now. It will be well to lay special stress on the progress of the institute since the last decree,[81] and also to state when it was obtained. The model and plan of approach to the Holy See will therefore be the same as in obtaining the previous decree, adding thereto any special suggestions that the Congregation of Religious thought expedient to ask for previously. It must be kept in mind that the more complete the document the greater likelihood there is for a speedy and favorable response and an avoidance of delays.

Finally a copy of the constitutions must be sent, unchanged from that exemplar previously inspected by the Holy See but incorporating those changes which were made in conformity with its expressed desire or permission. The same number of copies should be sent as before as the special commission will have to undertake the same routine work. If any difficulties that call for changes have been experienced in the constitution, or if the community has found it hard to live in accordance with the changes suggested by the Holy See, now is the apt

---

[80] *Normae* (1921), n. 9.

[81] Lanslots, *A Handbook of Canon Law*, p. 40.

time humbly to manifest these to the Sacred Congregation with the proper and just reasons why their observance is difficult or why the recommended changes are sought. Indications should also be given as to what the community wishes and how it desires the changes to be effected. Any such suggestions that are sent to the Apostolic See should be agreed upon by the chapter and even if any great changes are to be made it is not necessary to obtain the consent of the entire community through a vote. The wish, however, of the chapter must be expressed by a vote. These desired changes should be inserted in a separate petition and not in the constitutions proper.[91b] If serious corrections are demanded another delay may be felt but if not the corrections to be made will be indicated in the text, and under these circumstances the decree of approbation of the religious institute and the approbation of the constitutions will be given for the sake of experiment. It may be said here that the Sacred Congregation of Religious has examined the constitutions *ex officio* with a view to determine upon their final form.

This decree differs little in form from the previous decree of commendation. The changes made are in the word *laudavit* which is changed to *approbat et confirmat* and then are added the words ". . . SSmus, constitutiones, prout in correcto exemplari continentur, ad certum tempus, ex. gr. ad septennium, per modum experimenti, approbat atque confirmat."[92]

Juridically this decree does not in any way change the status of the community. The act of the Holy See is an indication of the honorable purpose of the institute, a judgment that those who are in this community are on the right path to perfection and lastly, that the Apostolic See has adjudged their purpose to be holy and declared that it will be for the sanctification of all who faithfully follow such a life. It is a great security and the community can now go onward with unfalter-

91b Cf. *A. A. S.* XIII (1921), 538.

92 *Normae* (1921), N. 20 b, n. 11.

ing steps, secure in the authority of the Sacred Congregation and the Pope.

As can readily be seen, exceptions from the ordinary mode of procedure may be made in any of these stages, as sometimes the decree of approbation of the institute is given when it first presents itself to the Apostolic See without being preceded by the decree of commendation. This happens when the institute is so favorably conditioned at the time of its coming before the Holy See that there is no reason for further delay.[93] But according to the *Normae* of 1901 the approbation of the constitutions for the sake of experiment is very rarely omitted.[94] It would seem that sometimes, though rarely, the constitutions are definitely approved when Rome first examines them.

III. *The Definite Approbation of the Constitutions.* This is the final and greatest seal of Rome's approval to the constitutions. The method of obtaining this approbation is by the identical process which was required in the other approbations.[95] The time for petitioning this, as is easily seen, is at the expiration of the time limit set when the constitutions were approved for the temporary period. There is no obligation however, to approach the Holy See at the end of that period although explanations may be in order in case a reason is asked to explain the delay. Any desirable and reasonable changes in the constitutions should be asked for now since this final approbation is to give a determined and lasting character to the constitutions, and in the form of this final approbation they are expected to be the permanent laws and the unchanging guide of the community. This definite approbation, as were the others, is obtained through the Congregation of Religious and although the act of that body receives the confirmation of the Supreme Pontiff, it proceeds chiefly from the Sacred Congregation.

[93] N. 12, *Normae* (1921).

[94] *Normae* (1921), N. 23.

[95] Lanslots, *A Handbook of Canon Law,* p. 42.

The directories, books of customs or private prayers that had been previously subjected to the examination of the Holy See may still be changed at the discretion of the new community since the Apostolic See inspected them but did not approve them.[96] But the superior or chapter can not change the constitutions as that right is reserved solely to the Holy See. The final act on the part of the Holy See relative to the institution has taken place and nothing remains to be done but the faithful and scrupulous observance of the rule. This does not in any way exclude the possibility of special occasions arising in the future which would call for a change in the constitutions, but these must be made in accordance with the procedure prescribed by law.

When it is said that this final approbation is the last thing that the community can desire no consideration is taken of another approbation which is in reality greater. This is the direct and personal approbation by the Pope through a brief or bull. This custom of having recourse to the Supreme Pontiff, for direct and personal approbation through a brief or bull, and once so frequent that all communities, at least those before the present growth of religious congregations, formerly received it, as seen in the various letters and documents of approbation, died out during the past century. But a glance over the last few years shows us that once more it is coming into vogue.[97] The number of religious congregations thus approved by special letter of the Pope shows how much this practice is growing. If these letters are examined the cause of the large number is found in the necessity that all religious institutes were under of revising their constitutions according to

[96] Vicente, *Inst. Rec.*, n. 126, p. 56; Lanslots, *op. cit.*, p. 40.

[97] Brief, "*Religiosorum virorum,*" March 20, 1928—*A. A. S.*, XX (1928), 224; brief, "*Francisci Salesii,*" January 29, 1928—*A. A. S.*, XX (1928), 250; brief, "*De regulari,*" July 20, 1926—*A. A. S.*, XIX (1927), 176; brief "*Sororum a S. Iosepho.*" August 5, 1925—*A. A. S.*, XVIII (1926), 125; brief "*Umbratilem,*" July 8, 1924—*A. A. S.*, XVI (1924), 385; brief "*Monachorum vita,*" August 20, 1924—*A. A. S.*, XVII (1925), 64.

the new canon law.[98] It was very becoming that these should be especially approved by His Holiness since their previous constitutions had been so approved, or otherwise the more recent approbation would seem to be of less importance than the old. Thus far those honored in this manner were old communities, practically all orders, though one religious congregation is also included. This is the Congregation of the Sisters of St. Joseph of Toronto, which though of recent origin in Canada yet traces its origin back several centuries.[99] Even with more modern communities, namely religious of simple vows, it can not be considered unbecoming that they aim at and strive for the greatest of all approbations, that done immediately by the Holy Father himself.[100] This approbation is what former writers called the solemn approbation of the constitution or rule.

Canonically it makes but little difference whether a religious institute receives the approval directly from the Pope or from the Congregation of Religious. Though the action of the Congregation of Religious is confirmed by the Pope, the act as such is the Congregation's and the effects of infallibility do not flow from it. When the Pope acts personally and approves and confirms most solemnly, his judgment then is infallible as was seen in an earlier chapter. Besides, and this is of value, the confirmation of the Congregation of Religious is an approbation *in forma communi*, whereas the confirmation of His Holiness is usually *in forma specifica*.[101] Practically there is not so much difference, yet it can not be doubted that a brief or bull of the Pope confers greater strength and stability besides bestowing the honor and dignity that flows from the authority of the Pope. This solemn form is recognized in the context and

[98] Decree of S. Cong. of Rel., *"Ad normam Canonis,"* June 26, 1918—A. A. S., X (1918), 290.

[99] *"Sororum a S. Iosepho,"* August 5, 1925—*A. A. S.*, XVIII (1926), 125.

[100] *Comm. pro Rel.*, IX (1928), 295.

[101] *Comm. pro Rel.*, IX (1928), 295; Cf. S. Cong. of Ep. & Reg.. rescript, *Pragen*, April 27, 1883—*A. S. S.*, XVI, 286, 293.

the tenor of the words and phrases used. This is easily seen from the words of one of the letters mentioned above. The decree of approbation is stated in these words: " . . .*motu proprio atque ex certa scientia et matura deliberatione Nostra, deque Apostolicae nostrae potestatis plenitudine, praesentium Litterarum tenore perpetuumque in modum, institutum Sororum a Sancto Joseph Torontinensium, uti Congregationem religiosam votorum simplicium, ac salva ad sacrorum canonum normam Ordinariorum iurisdictione, adprobamus et confirmamus.*"[102]

[102] "*Sororum a S. Iosepho,*" August 5, 1925—*A. A. S.*, XVIII (1926), 125.

Finis.

Bibliography

I SOURCES

Acta Apostolicae Sedis, Commentarium Officiale, Rome, 1909-
Acta et Decreta Concilii Plenarii Americae Latinae, 2 vols., Rome, 1902.
Acta et Decreta Sacrorum Conciliorum Recentiorum (Collectio Lacensis), 7 vols., Friburgi Brisgovae, 1870-1890.
Acta Sanctae Sedis, 41 vols., Rome, 1865-1908.
Basilica, Charles Heimbach, Leipzic, 1833.
Bizzarri, Andreas, *Collectanea in usum Secretariae Sacrae Congregationis Episcoporum et Regularium,* Romae, 1885.
Bullarii Romani Continuatio Summorum Pontificum, 19 vols., Prati, 1756-1883.
Bullarium Diplomatum et Privilegiorum Sanctorum Romanorum Pontificum, 24 vols., Turin, 1857-1872.
Codex Juris Canonici, Rome, 1919.
Codex Theodosianus, ed. P. Krueger, Th. Mommsen, P. M. Meyer, 3 vols., Berolini, 1905.
Codicis Iuris Canonici Fontes, cura Emi Petri Card. Gasparri editi, 5 vols., Rome, 1923-1929.
Collectanea S. Congregationis de Propaganda Fide, 2 vols., Rome, 1907.
Constitutiones Urbanae Ordinis Minorum Conventualium, Mechlin, 1880.
Corpus Juris Canonici, Richter, L. Aemilian, Leipzic, 1839.
Corpus Juris Civilis, Thead. Mommsen, ed. Berlin, 1922.
Denzinger, H.,—Bannwart, Clemens, *Enchiridion Symbolorum,* Friberg, 1913.
Mansi, John, *Sacrorum Conciliorum Nova et Amplissima Collectio,* 53 vols. Leipzic, 1903-1927.
Normae secundum quas S. Cong. Episcoporum et Regularium procedere solet in approbandis Novis Institutis votorum simplicium, Rome, 1901.
Schema Codicis Iuris Canonici, S. S. Domini Nostri Pii P. X., cum notis Petri Card. Gasparri, Rome, 1912.

WORKS OF REFERENCE

Angel de S. S. Corde, *Praelectiones Juris Canonici,* Paris, 1877.
Aquilar, Marian, *Scientiae Juridicae Compendium,* 2 ed., S. Dominici Calceatensis, 1904.
[Bachofen], Augustine, Charles, *A Commentary on the New Code of Canon Law,* 3 ed., 8 vols., St. Louis. 1921-1924.

[Bachofen], Augustine, Charles, *Rights and Duties of Ordinaries According to the Code and Apostolic Faculties*, St. Louis, 1924.

Ayrinhac, H. A., *Constitution of the Church in the New Code of Canon Law*, New York, 1925.

Benedict XIV, *De Synodo Dioecesana*, 2 vols., Venice, 1792.

Benedict XIV, olim Prosperi Card. Lambertini, *Institutiones Ecclesiasticae*, 3 vols., Louvain, 1762.

Blat, Albert, *Commentarium Textus Codicis Juris Canonici*, L. 1, Normae Generales, Rome, 1921.

Bonaventure, St., *Opera Omnia*, 10 vols., Quaracchi, 1882.

Bondini, P. Aloisius, *De Privilegio Exemptionis*, Romae, 1919.

Bouix, D., *Tractatus de Curia Romana*, Paris, 1859.

Bouix, D., *Tractatus de Jure Regularium*, 2 vols., Paris, 1882.

Brown, Brendan Francis, *The Canonical Juristic Personality*, Washington, D. C., 1927.

Cappello, Felix M., *Summa Iuris Publici Ecclesiastici*, 2 ed., Rome, 1928.

Catholic Encyclopedia, 17 vols., New York, 1907-1912.

Chelodi, John, *Jus de Personis*, Trent, 1925.

Cornely, R., *Cursus Scripturae Sacrae*, 46 vols., Paris, 1895-1913.

Currier, Charles, *History of Religious Orders*, New York, 1913.

[Brighton, de], Cuthbert, *Life of St. Francis of Assisi*, 2 ed., New York, 1925.

Fagnanus, Prosper, *Commentaria in Libros Decretalium*, 4 vols,, Venice, 1697.

Fanfani, Louis, *De Jure Religiosorum ad norman Codicis Juris Canonici*, Rome, 1920.

Ferraris, Lucius, *Bibliotheca Canonica*, 9 vols., Paris, 1886.

Forcellini, Aegidius, *Totius Latinitatis Lexicon*, 4 vols., Leipsic, 1831-1839.

Fortescue, Adrian, *The Orthodox Eastern Church*, 3 ed., London, 1911.

Funk, F. X., *A Manual of Church History*, 5 ed., St. Louis, 1910.

Hefele, C. J., *Conciliengeschichte*, 2 ed., 9 vols., Freiburg im Breisgau, 1873-1890.

Hefele, C. J., *History of the Councils of the Church* (T. C. Clark), 3 vols., Edinburgh, 1883.

Heimbucher, Max, *Die Orden und Kongregationen der katholischen Kirche*, 2 ed., 3 vols., Padedborn, 1907-1908.

Hurter, H., *Theologiae Dogmaticae Compendium in usum Studiosorum Theologiae*, 11 ed., Oeniponte, 1903.

Lanslots, D. I., *Handbook of Canon Law for Congregations of Women under Simple Vows*, 6 ed., New York, 1911.

Laurentius, Jos., *Institutiones Iuris Ecclesiastici*, 2 ed., Friberg, 1908.

Lucidi Angelus, *De Visitatione Sacrorum Liminum*, 3 vols., Rome, 1866.

Mazzella, Camillus, *De Religione et Ecclesia, Praelectiones Scholastico-Dogmaticae*, 5 ed., Rome, 1896.

Montalembert, Charles Comte, *Monks of the West*, 2 vols., New York, 1896.

New Catholic Dictionary, New York, 1929.

Ojetti, Benedict, S. J., *Synopsis Rerum Moralium et Juris Pontificii*, 3 ed., 4 vols., Rome, 1912.

Parsons, Rev. Reuben, *Studies in Church History*, 3 ed., 6 vols., Philadelphia, 1906.

Parsons, Wilfrid, S. J., *The Pope and Italy*, New York, 1929.

Pastor, Von Ludwig, *History of the Popes*, transl. by R. F. Kerr, 18 vols., St. Louis, 1906-1929.

Pejska, Joseph, *Jus Canonicum Religiosorum*, 3 ed., Friburgi Brisgovae, 1927.
Pesch, Christian, *Praelectiones Dogmaticae*, 5 ed., 6 vols., Friberg, 1915.
Philipps, George, *Compendium Juris Ecclesiastici*, ed. F. H. Vering, Ratisbon, 1875.
Piat, F. Montensis, *Praelectiones Juris Regularis*, 3 ed., 2 vols., Tornaci, 1906.
Raus, J. B., *De Sacrae Obedientiae Virtute et Voto*, Lyons, 1923.
Reinmann, Gerald Joseph, *The Third Order Secular of St. Francis*, Washington, 1928.
Rittershut, Conrad, *Expositio Methodica Novellarum Imp. Justiniani*, Florence, 1889.
Santi, Francis, *Praelectiones Juris Canonici quas juxta ordinem Decretalium Gregorii IX tradebat in scholis Pontif. Seminarii Romani Franciscus Santi*.....cura Martini Leitner, 3 ed., 5 vols., Ratisbon, 1898.
Schaefer, Timothy, *Compendium de Religiosis ad norman Codicis Juris Canonici*, Munster, 1927.
Schmalzgrueber, Francis, *Jus Canonicum Universum*, 12 vols., Rome, 1844.
Smith, S. B., *Compendium Juris Canonici*, New York, 1890.
Suarez, Francis, *Opera Omnia*, 26 vols., Paris, 1856-1861.
Tanquery, Ad., *Synopsis Theologiae Moralis et Pastoralis*, 9 ed., Rome, 1922.
Thomas, St., *Summa Theologica*, 6 vols., Turin, 1917.
Van Espen, Zegerus Bernard, *Opera Omnia*, 10 vols., Venice, 1769.
Vecchiotti, S. M., *Institutiones Canonicae*, 3 vols., Turin, 1886.
Verhoefen, Marian, *De Regularibus*, Louvain, 1846.
Vermeersch, A., *De Religiosis Institutis et Personis*, 2 vols., Rome, 1904.
Vermeersch, A., S. J., *De Religiosis et Missionariis, Supplementa et Monumenta Periodica*, 9 vols., Rome, 1911-1914.
Vermeersch, A., Creusen, J., *Epitome Juris Canonici*, 4 ed., 3 vols., Rome, 1929.
Vicente, Felix, *Recentia Instituta*, Madrid, 1916.
Vromant, G., *Jus Missionariorum*, T. II, De Personis, Louvain, 1929.
Wernz, F. X., *Jus Decretalium*, 2 ed., 6 vols., Rome, 1908.
Wernz-Vidal, Peter, *Jus Canonicum ad Codicis Normam Exactum*, T. II, *Personis*, 2 ed., Rome, 1928.
Zawart, Anscar, *The Capuchins, An Historical Survey*, Washington, 1928.
Zitelli, Zephyrin, *Apparatus Iuris Ecclesiastici*, Rome, 1886.

PERIODICALS

American Ecclesiastical Review, The, Philadelphia, 1889-
Annuario Pontificio, 1917, 1921.
Catholic Historical Review, Washington, 1915-
Catholic World, 1865-
Commentarium pro Religiosis, Publicatio mensilis opera et studio Missionariorum Filiorum Immac. Cordis B. V. M., Rome, 1920-
Jus Pontificium, ad canonicas disciplinas spectantes, Rome, 1921-
The Official Catholic Year Book, New York, 1928.

UNIVERSITAS CATHOLICA AMERICAE

WASHINGTONII, D. C.

FACULTAS IURIS CANONICI

1930-1931

No. 71.

TITULI

DEUS LUX MEA

THESES

QUAS

AD DOCTORATUS GRADUM

IN

JURE CANONICO

APUD UNIVERSITATEM CATHOLICAM AMERICAE

CONSEQUENDUM

PUBLICE PROPUGNABIT

CLEMENS RAYMUNDUS ORTH

SACERDOS ORDINIS MINORUM CONVENTUALIUM

LICENTIATUS IN JURE CANONICO

HORA IX A. M. DIE 28 MAII, A. D. MCMXXX

Tituli

DE IURE CANONICO

I.	De Dissertatione.	
II.	Canones 1-7	De Ambitu Codicis.
III.	Canones 8-24	De Legibus Ecclesiasticis.
IV.	Canones 25-30	De Consuetudine.
V.	Canones 31-35	De Temporis Supputatione.
VI.	Canones 36-62	De Rescriptis.
VII.	Canones 63-79	De Privilegiis.
VIII.	Canones 80-86	De Dispensationibus.
IX.	Canones 87-107	Generales Notiones de Personis.
X.	Canones 111-117	De Clericorum Adscriptione Alicui Dioecesi.
XI.	Canones 118-123	De Juribus et Privilegiis Clericorum.
XII.	Canones 124-144	De Obligationibus Clericorum.
XIII.	Canones 145-195	De Officiis Ecclesiasticis.
XIV.	Canones 196-210	De Potestate Ordinaria et Delegata.
XV.	Canones 211-214	De Reductione Clericorum ad Statum Laicalem.
XVI.	Canones 487-498	De Notione Religionis, et de Erectione et Suppressione Religionis, Provinciae et Domus.
XVII.	Canones 538-586	De Admissione in Religionem.
XVIII.	Canones 592-631	De Obligationibus et Privilegiis Religiosorum.
XIX.	Canones 820-823	De Tempore et Loco Missae Celebrandae.
XX.	Canones 824-844	De Missarum Eleemosynis seu Stipendiis.
XXI.	Canones 1012-1018	De Matrimonio in Genere.
XXII.	Canones 1019-1034	De iis quae Matrimonii Celebrationi Praemitti Debent.

XXIII.	Canones 1035-1057	De Impedimentis in Genere.
XXIV.	Canones 1058-1066	De Impedimentis Impedientibus.
XXV.	Canones 1067-1080	De Impedimentis Dirimentibus.
XXVI.	Canones 1081-1093	De Consensu Matrimoniali.
XXVII.	Canones 1094-1103	De Forma Celebrationis Matrimonii.
XXVIII.	Canones 1110-1117	De Matrimonii Effectibus.
XXIX.	Canones 1552-1568	De Notione Iudicii et de Foro Competenti.
XXX.	Canones 1569-1607	De Variis Tribunalium Gradibus et Speciebus.
XXXI.	Canones 1608-1645	De Disciplina in Tribunalibus Servanda.
XXXII.	Canones 1646-1666	De Partibus in Causa.
XXXIII.	Canones 1667-1705	De Actionibus et Exceptionibus.
XXXIV.	Canones 1706-1725	De Causae Introductione.
XXXV.	Canones 1726-1746	De Litis Contestatione, de Litis Instantia, et de Interrogationibus Partibus in Judicio Faciendis.
XXXVI.	Canones 1747-1836	De Probationibus.
XXXVII.	Canones 1837-1857	De Causis Incidentibus.
XXXVIII.	Canones 1858-1877	De Processus Publicatione, de Conclusione in Causa, de Causae Discussione, et de Sententia.
XXXIX.	Canones 2195-2198	De Natura Delicti Ejusque Divisione.
XL.	Canones 2199-2211	De Imputabilitate Delicti, de Causis Illam Aggravantibus vel Minuentibus et de Iuridicis Delicti Effectibus.
XLI.	Canones 2212-2213	De Conatu Delicti.
XLII.	Canones 2214-2240	De Poenis in Genere.
XLIII.	Canones 2241-2285	De Poenis Medicinalibus seu de Censuris.
XLIV.	Canones 2286-2305	De Poenis Vindicativis.
XLV.	Canones 2306-2313	De Remediis Poenalibus et Poenitentiis.

DE JURE ROMANO

XLVI.	Historical Periods of Roman Law.
XLVII.	The Sources of Roman Law.
XLVIII.	Personality.
XLIX.	Slavery.
L.	Citizenship.
LI.	Patria Potestas.

Vidit Facultas:

PHILIPPUS BERNARDINI, S.T.D., J.U.D., Decanus.
LUDOVICUS H. MOTRY, S.T.D., J.C.D., a Secretis.
VALENTINUS T. SCHAAF, O.F.M., J.C.D.
FRANCISCUS J. LARDONE, S.T.D., J.U.D.

Vidit Rector Magnificus Universitatis:
JACOBUS HUGO RYAN, Ph.D., S.T.D., LL.D., Litt.D.

Catholic University of America

CANON LAW STUDIES

1. Frebiks, Rev. Celestine A., C.PP.S., J.C.D., Religious Congregations in Their External Relations, 121 pp., 1916.
2. Galliher, Rev. Daniel M., O.P., J.C.D., Canonical Elections, 117 pp., 1917.
3. Borkowski, Rev. Aurelius L., O.F.M., J.C.D., De Confraternitatibus Ecclesiasticis, 136 pp., 1918.
4. Castillo, Rev. Cayo, J.C.D., Disertacion Historico-canonica sobre la Potestad del Cabildo en Sede Vacante o Impedida del Vicario Capitular, 99 pp., 1919 (1918).
5. Kubelbeck, Rev. William J., S.T.B., J.C.D., The Sacred Penitentiaria and Its Relations to Faculties of Ordinaries and Priests, 129 pp., 1918.
6. Petrovits, Rev. Joseph J. C., S.T.D., J.C.D., The New Church Law on Matrimony, X-461 pp., 1919.
7. Hickey, Rev. John J., S.T.B., J.C.D., Irregularities and Simple Impediments in the New Code of Canon Law, 100 pp., 1920.
8. Klekotka, Rev. Peter J., S.T.B., J.C.D., Diocesan Consultors, 179 pp., 1920.
9. Wannenmacher, Rev. Francis, J.C.D., The Evidence in Ecclesiastical Procedure Affecting the Marriage Bond, 1920. (Not Printed.)
10. Golden, Rev. Henry Francis, J.C.D., Parochial Benefices in the New Code, IV-119 pp., 1921. (Printed 1925).
11. Koudelka, Rev. Charles J., J.C.D., Pastors, Their Rights and Duties According to the New Code of Canon Law, 211 pp., 1921.
12. Melo. Rev. Antonius, O.F.M., J.C.D., De Exemptione Regularium, X-188 pp., 1921.
13. Schaaf, Rev. Valentine Theodore, O.F.M., S.T.B., J.C.D., The Cloister, X-180 pp., 1921.
14. Burke, Rev. Thomas Joseph, S.T.B., J.C.D., Competence in Ecclesiastical Tribunals, IV-117 pp., 1922.

15. LEECH, REV. GEORGE LEO, J.C.D., A Comparative Study of the Constitution "Apostolicae Sedis" and the "Codex Juris Canonici," 179 pp., 1922.

16. MOTRY, REV. HUBERT LOUIS, S.T.D., J.C.D., Diocesan Faculties according to the Code of Canon Law, II-167 pp., 1922.

17. MURPHY, REV. GEORGE LAWRENCE, J.C.D., Delinquencies and Penalties in the Administration and the Reception of the Sacraments, IV-121 pp., 1923.

18. O'REILLY, REV. JOHN ANTHONY, S.T.B., J.C.D., Ecclesiastical Sepulture in the New Code of Canon Law, II-129 pp., 1923.

19. MICHALICKA, REV. WENCESLAS CYRILL, O.S.B., J.C.D., Judicial Procedure in Dismissal of Clerical Exempt Religious, 107 pp. 1923.

20. DARGIN, REV. EDWARD VINCENT, S.T.B., J.C.D., Reserved Cases According to the Code of Canon Law, IV-108 pp., 1924.

21. GODFREY, REV. JOHN A., S.T.B., J.C.D., The Right of Patronage According to the Code of Canon Law, 153 pp., 1924.

22. HAGEDORN, REV. FRANCIS EDWARD, J.C.D., General Legislation on Indulgences, II-154 pp., 1924.

23. KING, REV. JAMES IGNATIUS, J.C.D., The Administration of the Sacraments to Dying Non-Catholics, V-141 pp., 1924.

24. WINSLOW, REV. FRANCIS JOSEPH, A.F.M., J.C.D., Vicars and Prefects Apostolic, IV-149 pp., 1924.

25. CORREA, REV. JOSE SERVELION, S.T.L., J.C.D., La Potestad Legislativa de la Iglesia Catolica, IV-127 pp., 1925.

26. DUGAN, REV. HENRY FRANCIS, M.A., J.C.D., The Judiciary Department of the Diocesan Curia, 87 pp., 1925.

27. KELLER, REV. CHARLES FREDERICK, S.T.B., J.C.D., Mass Stipends, 167 pp., 1925.

28. PASCHANG, REV. JOHN LINUS, J.C.D., The Sacramentals According to the Code of Canon Law, 129 pp. 1925.

29. PIONTEK, REV. CYRILLUS, O.F.M., S.T.B., J.C.D., De Indulto Exclaustrationis necnon Saecularizationis, XIII-289 pp., 1925.

30. KEARNEY, REV. RICHARD JOSEPH, S.T.B., J.C.D., Sponsors at Baptism According to the Code of Canon Law, IV-127 pp., 1925.

31. BARTLETT, REV. CHESTER JOSEPH, A.M., LL.B., J.C.D., The Tenure of Parochial Property in the United States of America, V-108 pp., 1926.

32. KILKER, REV. ADRIAN JEROME, J.C.D., Extreme Unction, V-425, pp., 1926.

33. MCCORMICK, REV. ROBERT EMMETT, J.C.D., Confessors of Religious, VIII-266 pp., 1926.

34. MILLER, REV. NEWTON THOMAS, J.C.D., Founded Masses According to the Code of Canon Law, VII-93 pp., 1926.

35. ROELKER, REV. EDWARD G., S.T.D., J.C.D., Principles of Privilege According to the Code of Canon Law, XI-166 pp., 1926.

36. Bakalarczyk, Rev. Richardus, M.I.C., J.U.D., De Novitiatu, VIII-208 pp., 1927.

37. Pizzuti, Rev. Lawrence, O.F.M., J.U.L., De Parochis Religiosis, 1927. (Not Printed.)

38. Bliley, Rev. Nicholas Martin, O.S.B., J.C.D., Altars According to the Code of Canon Law, XIX-132 pp., 1927.

39. Brown, Brendan Francis, A.B., LL.M., J.U.D., The Canonical Juristic Personality with Special Reference to its Status in the United States of America, V-212 pp., 1927.

40. Cavanaugh, Rev. William Thomas, C.P., J.U.D., The Reservation of the Blessed Sacrament, VIII-101 pp., 1927.

41. Doheny, Rev. William J., C.S.C., A.B., J.U.D., Church Property: Modes of Acquisition, X-118 pp., 1927.

42. Feldhaus, Rev. Aloysius H., C.PP.S., J.C.D., Oratories IX-141 pp., 1927.

43. Kelly, Rev. James Patrick, A.B., J.C.D., The Jurisdiction of the Simple Confessor, X-208 pp., 1927.

44. Neuberger, Rev. Nicholls, J., J.C.D., Canon 6 or the Relation of the Codex Juris Canonici to the Preceding Legislation, V-95 pp., 1927.

45. O'Keeffe, Rev. Gerald Michael, J.C.D., Matrimonial Dispensations, Powers of Bishops, Priests, and Confessors, VIII-232 pp., 1927.

46. Quigley, Rev. Joseph, A.M., A.B., J.C.D., Condemned Societies, 139 pp., 1927.

47. Zaplotnik, Rev. Ioannes Leo, J.C.D., De Vicariis Foraneis, X-142, 1927.

48. Duskie, Rev. John Aloysius, A.B., J.C.D., The Canonical Status of the Orientals in the United States, VIII-196 pp., 1928.

49. Hyland, Rev. Francis Edward, J.C.D., Excommunication, Its Nature, Historical Development and Effects, VIII-181 pp., 1928.

50. Reinmann, Rev. Gerald Joseph, O.M.C., J.C.D., The Third Order Secular of Saint Francis, 201 pp., 1928.

51. Schenk, Rev. Francis J., J.C.D., The Matrimonial Impediments of Mixed Religion and Disparity of Cult. XVI-318 pp., 1929.

52. Coady, Rev. John Joseph, S.T.D., J.U.D., A.M., The Appointment of Pastors, VIII-150 pp., 1929.

53. Kay, Rev. Thomas Henry, J.C.D., Competence in Matrimonial Procedure, VIII-164 pp., 1929.

54. Turner, Rev. Sidney Joseph, C.P., J.U.D., The Vow of Poverty, XLIX-217 pp., 1929.

55. Kearney, Rev. Raymond A., A.B., S.T.D., J.C.D., The Principles of Delegation, VII-149 pp., 1929.

56. Conran, Rev. Edward James, A.B., J.C.D., The Interdict, V-163 pp., 1930.

57. O'Neill, Rev. William H., J.C.D., Papal Rescripts of Favor, VII-219 pp., 1930.

58. Bastnagel, Rev. Clement Vincent, J.U.D., The Appointment of Parochial Adjutants and Assistants, XV-262 pp., 1930.

59. Ferry, Rev. William A., A.B., J.C.D., Stole Fees, X-108 pp., 1930.

60. Costello, Rev. John Michael, A.B., J.C.D., Domicile and Quasi-Domicile, VII-201 pp., 1930.

61. Kremer, Rev. Michael Nicholas, A.B., S.T.B., J.C.D., Church Support in the United States, VI-137 pp., 1930.

62. Angulo, Rev. Luis, C.M., J.C.L., Legislación de la Iglesia Católica sobre la Intención en la Aplicación de la Misa, 1931.

63. Frey, Rev. Wolfgang, O.S.B., A.B., J.C.L., The Act of Religious Profession, 1931.

64. Roberts, Rev. James Brendan, A.B., J.C.L., The Banns of Marriage, 1931.

65. Ryder, Rev. Raymond Aloysius, A.B., J.C.L., Simony, 1931.

66. Campagna, Rev. Michael Angelo, Ph.B., J.U.L., Il Vicario Generale del Vescovo, 1931.

67. Cox, Rev. Joseph Godfrey, A.B., J.C.L., The Administration of Seminaries, 1931.

68. Gregory, Rev. Donald Joseph, S.T.B., J.U.L., The Pauline Privilege, 1931.

69. Donohue, Rev. John Francis, A.M., J.C.L., The Impediment of Crime, 1931.

70. Dooley, Eugene, O.M.I., J.C.L., The Cult of Relics, 1931.

71. Orth, Rev. Clement Raymond, O.M.C., J.C.L., The Approbation of Religious Institutes, 1931.

Vita

Raymond Aloysius Orth was born in Kenosha, Wisconsin, April 12, 1899. His primary education was obtained from the Sisters of St. Francis at St. Aemilian's Orphan Home in St. Francis, Wisconsin. In September, 1914, he entered St. Francis Seminary where he remained until 1918. In this year he entered the novitiate of the Order of Friars Minor Conventual, taking the name of Clement. He was professed in the Order August 17, 1919, and entered the Seminary of the Order at St. Anthony-on-Hudson, Rensselaer, N. Y., where he completed his course in Philosophy and Theology. Here on June 14, 1924 he was ordained to the Holy Priesthood. In September of that same year he entered the graduate School of Canon Law at the Catholic University of America in Washington, D. C., and in the following June received the degree of Licentiate in Canon Law. From 1925-1929 he was professor of Astronomy, Geology, and Instrumental Music at Mt. St. Francis Pro-Seminary at Floyds Knobs, Ind. In September 1929 he again matriculated at the Catholic University in Washington and in partial fulfillment of the requirements for the degree of Doctor in Canon Law, he wrote this dissertation.

www.ingramcontent.com/pod-product-compliance
Lightning Source LLC
LaVergne TN
LVHW050227080826
844660LV00012B/489

* 9 7 8 0 8 1 3 2 2 2 6 0 8 *